TREES FOR TOMORROW

TREES FOR
Tomorrow

By Frank Lockyear & Robert Gray

WRS
PUBLISHING

A Division of WRS Group, Inc.
Waco, Texas

First published in the United States of America in 1993 by WRS Publishing, A Division of WRS Group, Inc., 701 N. New Road, Waco, Texas 76710
Front cover photo by Robert Gray
Book design by Kenneth Turbeville
Cover design by Talmage Minter
Back cover illustration by Joe James

10 9 8 7 6 5 4 3 2 1

Library of Congress Cataloging-in-Publication Data

Lockyear, Frank, 1913-
    Trees for tomorrow / by Frank Lockyear & Robert Gray.
        p.   cm.
    ISBN 1-56796-019-7 : $12.95
    1. Lockyear, Frank, 1913-   . 2. Nursery growers—Oregon—Biography.
3. Tree planters (Persons)—Oregon—Biography. 4. Tree planting.
5. ReTree International. 6. Trees. I. Gray, Robert, 1922-   . II Title.
SB63.L55A3   1993
333.75'153'092—dc20
    [B]   93-28009
                                                               CIP

Dedicated to the future of forests
throughout the world and to
John, Sally, Richard, and Victoria

Table of Contents

Introduction

On a wet afternoon in mid-December 1990, I was sitting at a window in the monastery of Simonos Petra, looking out at the worst storm to hit northern Greece in more than fifty years. It was a real gully washer. The torrents of rain didn't *fall*; they were whipped across the sky on gale-force winds. They splattered against the window, patterning the glass with swirling loops and streamers of water. Trying to see out that window was like looking through a lace curtain. The wind raised the planks lying on the temporary scaffolding outside the window and scooted them around as though they were cardboard. I prayed they didn't go flying; those planks were my access to the bathroom.

The wind carried the rain across the monolith called Simon's Rock—Simonos Petra—for which the monastery is named and on which it and everything in it, including me, were perched. The deluge smashed against the bare hillside beyond. It tore away the bare topsoil, turning it into thick, brown gravy that flooded down the slope. At the cliff edge it plunged eight hundred feet straight down into the Aegean Sea.

The storm had continued unabated for the four days I had been at Simonos Petra, penning me inside. I hadn't traveled halfway around the world to sit at this window. Yet here I was, spending my time sleeping, eating, going to church, meeting monastery officials, and inching my way along those planks as necessary. Mainly though, I just sat looking out at the rain.

In a small shed at the monastery's entrance, there were ten boxes of California redwood seedlings, a total of four thousand trees. We were at Simonos Petra to deliver them to the monastery's foresters, and to help plant them. I had chaperoned those redwood seedlings eight thousand miles from Oregon. They had been trucked from nurseries in California to my home in Oregon where they were poked and prodded by Oregon agricultural inspectors, and crammed into the baggage compartment of the SAS DC-10 that carried us over the Pole to Copenhagen. They had accompanied our party across Europe to Athens, where matters could have gotten a bit sticky.

Greek agricultural officials weren't particularly sympathetic about allowing four thousand aliens into the country, even if they were just trees. I tried to explain that the State of Oregon had certified them as free from pathogens, but Customs didn't understand English, and I didn't speak Greek. Gridlock. A member of our party saved the situation.

Father Sergios, pastor of the Three Saints Orthodox Church in Unalaska, Alaska, and fluent in Greek, gently but firmly took command. After some heated conversation, the trees were cleared and put aboard the Olympia Airlines plane for Thesaloniki. There they languished for two days in a shaded corner of the Thessaloniki Agricultural and Industrial Institute, more commonly known as the American Farm School, where the school's director, George Draper, graciously put us up while we waited for further clearance papers. When we got clearance for the monastery, we took the trees to the bus station and piled them on the sidewalk. There were many passengers with much luggage lined up for the bus, and that bus was very small. The driver, the ticket agent, and the other people looked at our pile of boxes and shook their heads. They began talking and pointing at the boxes. The noise level gradually rose. The men waved their arms and yelled at each other. They measured and remeasured the boxes. They ended up face-to-face, screaming. The other passengers pointed at *their* bags and started to scream. Matters were beginning to look shaky.

"Why is everybody angry? Why are they fighting?" I asked Father Sergios.

"What anger? What fighting?" Father Sergios asked calmly. "They are simply discussing how best to pack the boxes on the bus."

In predawn darkness our ten boxes of trees were on the bus with us and headed down the road to Ouranoupolis, port of departure for Mt. Athos, the Holy Mountain, and site of the monastery of Simonos Petra. At Ouranoupolis they were transferred to a ferry that looked like a relic from the second World War. Two hours down the coast they were offloaded, stuffed into a Land Rover and trundled up a trail that was about to be washed off its tenuous hold on a cliff.

Now the trees were still in their boxes in a shed in one of the most isolated places in the world. The boxes hadn't even been opened, and from the looks of things, they wouldn't be for a long time. The jeep trail was washed out. The one phone line was down. Simonos Petra was as cut off from the world as it had been when it was established almost a thousand years earlier.

So on our last day I sat by the window watching the rain. I didn't want to think about the scramble down the narrow path that switch-backed down the cliff face to the shore. I didn't want to think about what that scramble would do to a pair of hips that had seen far better days. I didn't want to think about the long wait we might have until a ferry came by. I didn't want to think about the long, long trip home. As I sat there looking out on the worst storm to hit northern Greece in half a century, all I could think about were those four thousand California redwood seedlings still in their boxes at the monastery's entrance.

A person might understandably be confused about why a seventy-seven year old retired nurseryman from Wilsonville, Oregon, would travel halfway around the world just to plant four thousand *Sequoia semperviren* seedlings at an eleventh-century Greek Orthodox monastery. All I can say is that that, plus a few other matters having to do with trees, the planet, our stewardship of it, and how I see my role in all of this, is what this book is about.

Chapter 1

They say it takes an optimist to plant a tree. If that's so, I guess I'm one of the world's most dedicated optimists, since I've been planting trees for more than sixty years. When I was a kid in the Boy Scouts, I went out with the troop to plant them. Later a large part of one of my first jobs was working with trees. Then in the nursery and landscape business that I set up and ran for thirty-five years, trees represented a major part of my income. And for the past nineteen years, they have filled just about all my waking hours.

For a person so involved with trees and all of nature, I was born and grew up in exactly the right place, the Pacific Northwest. Even now, with half a dozen major cities rising where forests once grew, and hundreds of suburbs clustered around them, nature is the biggest, most obvious facet of the region. It is all around you, no matter where you are. In the most crowded part of Seattle or Portland, all you have to do is look up, and there are the mountains—the Olympics, the Cascades, Mts. Rainier, St. Helens, Hood—riding the skyline. A few minutes drive takes you out of the city and into some of the most beautiful country in the world. Anybody who has the privilege of growing up here is indeed a blessed person.

I was also blessed in the parents I was given. They were farm people who came west from southern Indiana around the turn of the century. For those times they had good educations. My mother went to high school, which was considered unusual for a farm girl. My father passed the test to attend West Point, but was beaten out in the actual appointment by the nephew of the state's governor. Rank has its privileges. My father's brother, Elmer, attended Vanderbilt and later became a probate judge in Evansville, Indiana. His grandson now has the same job in the same town.

My father's name was Edward, Edward Lockyear. He died on the Fourth of July, 1950, at about age eighty, from uremic poisoning. My mother's name was Minnie. She lived 101 years and eight months, and was up and about on the last day of her life. She lived with two of my sisters, but still prepared meals and helped take care of the house and garden. Then one day she simply sat down on the steps and died. Her mother had lived to be ninety-eight, and her grandmother, 104. Their family name was Henn. They had come from Germany and settled in Indiana about fifteen miles from Evansville. I suppose they spoke German in the home, because my mother was fluent in the language.

When my parents decided to come west, they chose the Portland area because they had friends here. My mother told me stories about that train trip from Indiana. She said that, before they left, she prepared baskets of food for the five-day trip. Five days! There were about four children by then, plus the two adults, so those baskets must have been bulging. At Kelso, Washington, downstream from Portland, the tracks ended. There was no bridge across the Columbia River. The train was rolled onto a barge and towed to the Oregon side, where it was put back on tracks for the rest of the trip.

The family stayed in Portland for a few years, getting their feet on the ground. I hadn't been born yet, but other babies came along each year or so. By the time the family was completed, there were twelve children.

My father went to work for the Inman-Poulson Lumber Mill in Portland. He was put on the green gang, the men who cut the raw logs as they entered the mill. It was really a tough job. In those days there was no union. My father had to work hard and fast, sixteen hours a day. The family lived not too far from the mill, and at the end of his shift, my father would walk or run home, get in a few hours of sleep, and then head back.

In those days Portland was the largest producer of lumber products of any city in the world. Even later, when I was growing up, there were many mills up and down the waterfront. All that is gone now. In fact, each year the number of mills throughout the Pacific Northwest is shrinking. Some people blame the environmental movements, especially the one to protect the northern spotted owl, but that's too simple. The reasons for the loss of jobs and mill closures go far beyond that one bird. Mills have become increasingly automated, with a resulting loss of jobs. And raw logs are being shipped overseas for processing. To get some idea of how much timber leaves this country, a person need only drive to just one port, Longview, Washington, a few miles downriver from Portland on the Columbia. He'll see acres of cold decks— as stacks of timber are called—waiting to be put aboard ships bound for Asia, millions and millions of board feet of timber waiting to be shipped overseas. Those logs will never go through an American mill. But many of them will come back to this country in the form of finished wood products.

In 1905, the city of Portland put on a magnificent exposition honoring the centennial of the Lewis and Clark expedition. That trip of exploration marked the opening of the land purchased by the United States from France in 1803. The Portland region, at the confluence of two major, navigable rivers, was to become the focus of the newly acquired land in the Northwest. So Lewis and Clark are important parts of the city's history. On the occasion of the centenary of their trip of exploration, Portland went all-out. I suppose it will again in 2005. With good fortune, and drawing on the genes I seem to have inherited from my mother's side of the family, I might be around to take part in it. If so, my main contribution to the shindig will be to have a huge tree planting.

As part of the 1905 Lewis and Clark Exposition, Portland constructed a building in which to house a forestry exhibit. Most of the Exposition buildings didn't last much beyond 1905, but that enormous log cabin—at twenty thousand

square feet the largest log building in the world—was a
Portland landmark until the mid-1960s, when it burned.
Some of the logs in the cabin were more than six feet in
diameter and weighed more than thirty tons.

There are very few trees that size left in unprotected
parts of the Pacific Northwest. The ancient forests they
lived in have been heavily logged for the past century,
and what is left is the subject of great controversy. The
wood products industry insists that these trees are mature
and will simply rot and be wasted if they are not harvested.
People on the other side argue that the progression of
trees from seedlings through maturity to old age and
death is no waste, simply natural processes that are
essential to the health of the forest. The ancient forests
still standing represent less than ten percent of those
which once grew here. As I'm writing this, there seems to
be a great deal of heat, and relatively little light, being
focused on the issue. The battle goes on, and who knows
where or when it will be resolved.

Because my father was essentially a farmer, he was also
a jack-of-all-trades. Any farmer worth his salt is. So, among
other things, he was a very good carpenter. During the
preparations for the Exposition, he quit the mill and went
to work on the Forestry building. He probably made more
money doing that than at the lumber mill, but, that
wasn't saying much. The wages for tradesmen were
pitifully low in those days.

Those low wages, plus horrible working conditions,
gave rise to the emerging labor movement in the
Northwest. One of the new unions, the Industrial Workers
of the World, popularly known simply as the IWW,
became active in the trades. The IWW held radical ideas
for the times—an eight-hour day, decent working
conditions, paid vacations, and so forth. A few years later,
it became quite a power, and in 1917 called a strike that
shut down logging throughout the Northwest. But the
country was about to enter World War I, and the army
needed huge amounts of spruce to build airplanes. So the
IWW was put out of business, and many of its leaders

were thrown in jail. The irony is that the Army formed a company union that brought about the very changes the IWW had struggled so hard for.

But in 1905, when the biggest log building in the world was being built on the Lewis and Clark Exposition grounds, the union was barely getting started and had hardly any power. It tried to organize the tradesmen on the Exposition project, with little success. It was an annoyance though, and the organizers apparently harassed employees. The city had too much money invested in the Exposition to tolerate any slowdown of work. City fathers were determined to open the Exposition on schedule, so they provided police protection for key workers. My father told me stories of being escorted back and forth between home and work by an officer.

The Lewis and Clark Centennial Exposition opened on schedule, and Portland got a major boost as a city on the move.

Shortly after the job at the Exposition grounds ended, the family decided that city life was not for them. They were, after all, farmers. They learned of land that was available in eastern Oregon, where the government had a new irrigation project on the Deschutes River. The Homestead Act of 1862 provided 160 acres of federal land to anyone who would live on it and farm it for five years. The family filed on a parcel near Redmond, Oregon, and settled in. I guess things were going along pretty well at first, but a few years later my father was kicked in the face by a wild horse he was breaking. It almost killed him, and for the rest of his life he was bothered by headaches.

Because he couldn't work that 160 acres any more, he moved the family to a small parcel of land near Sheridan, south of Portland. I was born there on August 10, 1913, the ninth in that family of twelve children—seven boys, five girls. There are still five of us living.

Looking back on those days, I suppose the Sheridan place was not a good farm or even much of a place to live. The house was just an old, single-wall building without any insulation. It was really quite an ordeal to keep it warm in the winter when the temperature sank below freezing and the wind was howling through all the cracks. But it was the first home I knew, the place where I learned to be a part of nature. And I have wonderful memories of it.

The house sat on top of a small hill. We had a little barn, a well, and a garden of sorts. There was one of the most wonderful views a person could imagine, a sweeping panorama of the central and northern Oregon volcanic peaks that rise along the Cascade skyline. Mts. St. Helens, Hood, Jefferson, and Adams; Three Sisters, and Three Finger Jack. About three o'clock in the afternoon, in summer, no matter how hot the day, we got a sea breeze from over the Coast Range, which lasted into the evening and cooled things down.

In springtime the house was surrounded by wildflowers. There was a kind of golden lily we called Lamb's Tongue, that grew about ten inches to a foot tall. We had a flower known as Shooting Star and another we called Indian Pink. There was a brown lily whose name I don't remember. Acres of wildflowers. Of course, that was only because that region hadn't been farmed yet. Farming eliminates a lot of nature—wildflowers, plants and shrubs—and when you fence a farm and turn livestock in, especially sheep and goats, they will destroy every growing thing. Today, the Sheridan region is filled with farms.

My brother Ralph was just two years younger than I, so we sort of grew up together. Being poor farm kids, whatever entertainment we had, we had to invent. Of course, out there in the country just about all of it took place out of doors.

One time Ralph and I were wandering around the barn and found a nest of rotten eggs. We had had some experience with rotten eggs before and knew that when they were really old and very rotten, if you threw them against a hard surface, they would sort of explode and fling that rotten stuff around. Well, I figured if we mixed up all kinds of grease and oil with the rotten stuff in those eggs, we might get a *really* big explosion. I didn't consider that I might go up along with it. So Ralph and I got some flammables we found around the farm— benzene, ether, creosote, crankcase oil, gasoline, axle grease, some kerosene. We ended up with a five-gallon bucket of the stuff. We took a pail of rotten eggs and the mixture out onto the dirt road in front of the farm, which seemed a good place for the experiment.

But then it occurred to me that a car might come along.

"Ralph," I said, "If our explosion goes off it might damage a car and we'd get in trouble."

So we decided to use the stubble field. It was a hot, dry day in late summer, the driest part of the year. We put the eggs and what we figured would be the explosives in the stubble and lit a match. But things didn't work out quite as we hoped. The mixture didn't explode. It just burned, *really* burned. So did the stubble. In short order we had a wildfire on our hands. I tried to stomp it out, and called for Ralph to help me.

He shook his head. "No. I'm not going to help you. I've got new shoes on and I'm not going to get them dirty."

I took off for home, screaming *"Fire! Fire!"*

My mother and sisters dashed from the house, saw what was happening, and went to the well for water. They filled some five-gallon buckets, soaked some burlap sacks, then ran into the stubble field and smothered the flames. The house was saved, and brother Ralph and I were sent to bed. I expected to get a whipping. Usually for something as wild and drastic as this, my dad would use a switch on me, which sharpened me up a bit. But I don't remember getting so much as a scolding for the fire. Ralph and I spent the rest of the day, all that night, and most of the following day, in bed.

I didn't have to depend on Ralph's help to get into mischief. I was pretty much able to do it all by myself. For instance, there was the wagon that my dad hitched the team up to. He maneuvered it by pushing and turning the tongue. I watched him do it often enough, and one day I decided to try it. The wagon was a big, heavy rig, but even as a little boy I was able to get it moving. I tugged on the tongue and got the wagon headed downhill. Then it took off on its own! I couldn't stop it, and had to jump out of the way. The wagon ended up rolling over a new plow my dad had, and breaking the shear. I don't remember if I got my bottom burned over this little adventure, but most likely I did.

When you grew up in the country in my time, you learned how to deal with livestock, and I learned how to milk the hard way. I had watched my mother milking our cow and figured that I could do this, too. So all by myself I brought up the stool and a pail and set to work. The problem was that I was working from the cow's offside. My mother milked from the cow's left side, I was on the right, and the cow didn't understand. She kicked me across the shed. I don't remember being badly hurt, but it was an effective lesson in how not to handle animals.

I guess I was always up to something or other. For instance, there were a lot of yellow jackets around the house. These bees are especially mean and seem to delight in stinging. I never got sick from their stings, but several members of my family did. So I took it on myself to get rid of the yellow jackets. Unlike certain other species of bees, yellow jackets live in underground nests. So on summer evenings, after they were back below the surface, I'd try to get them. I took a mattock or grub hoe and went out with my brother Ralph and sister Emily to destroy a nest. I dug really fast for a few seconds, then, just before the bees came boiling out, mad as hornets, the three of us started running. We ran up into the barn hayloft to get away, but some of the bees followed and the three of us thrashed around pounding bees out of our hair and screaming as they stung us. It was a war that never ended.

Not all the bees were yellow jackets. I remember an incident that happened in 1919 or '20. Near the Harmony School which we children attended, there was a large Douglas fir tree. A storm split off one of the branches, and the school children discovered that it was filled with wild honey. Many of us took honey home in our lunch boxes for several days.

That old schoolhouse was way out in the country, and the first-grade children got out earlier than the others. One afternoon, just as I got out, I saw an airplane flying overhead. An airplane! This was really an exciting event back in 1919. I came running back to school, screaming and shouting. "An airplane! An airplane!" The teacher let all the children out of school so they could come outside and catch a glimpse of the airplane I had spotted.

It didn't take much to supply excitement in those days. It might be a new car puttering along the dirt roads. Or that airplane, so rare that children got out of school to see it. Life went on pretty slowly.

In the seventy years since those days at Harmony, I've pretty much traveled around this world. I've worked with children, tens of thousands of them. Some of them were what a person might call well-off. Others were poor, dirt poor. But all those children seemed to be able to draw happiness from just being alive, especially when we were together planting trees in the outdoors. There is something about being out in nature that children, almost without exception, respond to.

Of course I'm not referring to those parts of the world where extreme poverty and the diseases that go with it are the normal way of life. It is impossible to be very happy when you are starving to death. But just thinking back on my own childhood, you really don't realize you are poor until you compare your situation with that of somebody better off. And you can find happiness in the simplest of things, like trying to explode rotten eggs, or finding a honey tree. It's too bad children of today, growing up in big cities, don't have access to such simple pleasures. But they don't, and part of our responsibility as adults is to expose them as closely as possible, to something comparable. Tree planting can do that.

Early in this century, illnesses were a more serious matter than they are now, as we didn't have good medicines and there weren't many doctors. Right after World War I, there was a lot of flu going around, and we got it. Doctor Roscoe Field came out to help us. He gave my oldest brother, Will, a prescription of Epsom salts. He was to take a rousing dose in water every half hour. If you are aware of how Epsom salts affects the human body, you can imagine the many, many trips Will made to the outhouse, or how many somebody had to make with the slop jar.

My brother Fred came down with the flu and was put in bed. One day while he was still sick, I was playing in the yard with two of my sisters, Emily and Mary. We had a hay rack in the barnyard for hauling hay behind a team. I was climbing on it and slipped. My whole body, except my head, went through the opening between the boards, leaving me hanging by my chin. Fred had to get out of his sick bed to lift me from the hay rack.

About 1923, there was a bad winter for our family. I brought home scarlet fever from school. Glen Hill, who sat next to me in the double seat, had had the sickness, and came back to school too soon. So I caught it and brought it home. Then it got passed around to the rest of our family, and the youngest of the children, Ben, died. That was a bad period. We lived in that poorly heated house, eating poor food, with hardly any wood at all to burn. It was really the worst time of our growing up that I can remember. I got over the fever first and was able to help keep the fire going in the kitchen, and take the slop jars to the outhouse.

Chapter 2

    Living in the country in the Pacific Northwest, I became aware of trees at a very early age. The mountains were covered by forests of Douglas fir, red cedar, and hemlock, and the valleys were thick with fruit and nut orchards. In a child's way, I sensed something of their magnificence, of their soul. I could spend hours at a time simply walking through the forests.

    Trees figured heavily in our lives. We burned firewood, of course, and my dad and older brothers used tree parts to make tools and implements. They fabricated wagon tongues and replacement handles for axes and hammers and other tools.

    Our little farm was surrounded by Garry oaks (*Quercus garrayana*), gnarled, rugged trees. Some of them were very large, maybe three feet in diameter. This is a tree of open parklands. I'm told the reason we had conditions favorable for oaks around the farm was that, long ago, the Indians who lived in that valley burned the coniferous forests to provide sunlight for grass that fed game animals the people hunted.

    My father used to cut oak trees for fence posts, and sometimes those posts actually sprouted and began growing. Two of my older brothers cut oak cordwood. They worked all day felling, bucking, and splitting those tough old trees, and all they got for their efforts was one dollar a cord. A cord of wood is a stack four feet wide, four feet tall and eight feet long—128 cubic feet of wood. It takes many hours to convert standing trees into cordwood. In those days, my brothers didn't even have the advantage of using chain saws. It was all hard, grueling handwork.

The mountains behind us held great forests of commercial-grade conifers, and they were heavily logged. Some of my very early recollections are of logging trucks pounding along on the road in front of our house. I suppose those trucks were a lot smaller than today's big diesel rigs, but to a small child they seemed enormous. They had solid rubber tires that made a great noise and kicked up clouds of dust. They terrified the cows as we took them along the road to the creek for water. When we heard the sirens those logging trucks carried, we'd drive our cows off the road as fast as we could.

Not all the logs were taken from the woods on trucks. There was a timber flume behind our little one-room schoolhouse, and I remember watching the activity in it. The flume ran from logging areas in the mountains down to the mill. All day long, cants would come floating along, splashing water over the sides and making an unholy racket as they bumped into each other and rammed against the sides of the flume. (A cant is a partially milled log.) Out there in the mountains when I was a boy, cants were milled from the logs well upstream near logging operations, then floated down to the finishing mill miles downstream.

The last functioning timber flume in the United States was operated by the Broughton Lumber Company in southwestern Washington, just a few miles upstream on the Columbia from Portland. It operated for sixty-six years, from 1920 until 1988, when diesel trucks made it obsolete. Cants were dumped in the flume beginning at seven o'clock each workday morning, and one hour later the first were taken out at the remanufacturing mill, eleven miles and 1,250 feet lower than where they were put in. During its operating life, the Broughton Lumber Company's flume carried 1.75 billion board feet of wood. Today, remnants of the flume can be seen hanging from the cliff face on the Washington side of the Columbia.

As a lifelong Oregonian, I remember how important that flume was to the economy of the region. The timber industry was, and still is, a major part of our economic base.

It will continue to be, because there is no questioning the fact that wood will remain an integral part of human activity.

Even in today's world, with all its plastics and metals, there are more than five thousand uses for wood and its byproducts. It is the most versatile building material we have. It can be worked with the simplest of tools. It can be fastened with something as simple as a nail, or as sophisticated as the most modern adhesives.

Pound for pound, wood is stronger than steel. Its compression strength is remarkable, although understandable, since this is what has to take the huge loads that press downward when a tree is standing. A one-inch-square block of Douglas fir two and a half inches tall, weighing just three-quarters of an ounce, can support a load of five tons.

Wood burns easily and sends off large amounts of heat. A pound of green (wet) wood produces forty-four hundred BTU's, and an equal amount of dry wood, 7,310. We humans have used wood as a basic fuel for thousands of years, and most people in the Third World still do. About one-half of the wood cut today is used as fuel, either directly or after being converted into charcoal.

Although wood burns well, the larger the piece, the more resistant it is to burning. This is because a heavy beam exposed to fire will char on the outside first, which insulates the interior, and leaves the beam stronger than a steel beam of comparable size. A steel beam heated to seventeen hundred degrees Farenheidt can't even support its own weight.

Dry wood is an excellent thermal and electrical insulator. However, the higher the moisture content, the poorer the insulating factor. Dry wood can last almost indefinitely. Wooden objects, all in good condition, have been taken from Egyptian tombs, and solid timbers more than twenty-seven hundred years old have been found in Turkish tombs. At the other extreme, if wood is kept fully submerged, it will also last indefinitely. The remains of nine-thousand-year-old wooden villages in good condition have been found underwater in Swiss lakes.

Wood is still the principal structural material for houses and other buildings, especially in those parts of the world that have forests. And even where the structure is made of other materials, wood is often used in the finish work— panels, stairs, moldings, and so forth. Wood is also used in the manufacture of many musical instruments—violins, guitars, pianos, and the like.

There is a story about Antonio Stradivari, whose violins are considered among the finest ever made. It is said that he would go into the woods near his home each spring to find the trees with the straightest grain. He would take along a mallet and hit each prospective tree until he found those with the best resonance. These were marked for felling. Stradivari is said to have searched for hardwood trees growing in the shade of other trees, since they supposedly had the straightest, longest grain.

Some people insist that the story is all hogwash, and that Stradivari didn't know any more about wood than he did about the varnishes he used to finish his instruments, which was said to be practically nothing. The truth, according to the skeptics, is that wood for Stradivarius violins came from trees that had floated in the millponds of Venice for years. Being immersed had hardened the resins, making the wood resonant.

When I was a boy and automobiles were just starting to make a widespread appearance, automobile wheels were made with wooden spokes. Of course, farm wagons and buggies had wooden wheels, too.

The wheel is thought to have been invented by nomadic tribes in Central Asia long before human history began to be recorded. Probably those first wheels were just slabs of wood fastened together by bronze or copper straps and hacked into a rough circle. They must have been heavy and awkward, and eventually were replaced by lightweight spoke wheels that had wooden rims and metal tires. Wheels were used extensively in Europe and Asia, but didn't appear in the New World until the European conquerors brought them.

The Aztecs and Mayas knew about the circle, but didn't

make the association between it and a means to carry a load. They did use the circle as a calendar, though, and it was more accurate than those in use elsewhere in the world at the time.

We have used wood in shipbuilding for countless centuries. A vessel built from Lebanese cedar was dug up from a pit near the Great Pyramid of Giza in 1954. More than twenty-five hundred years earlier, it had been buried there as the funeral ship for the pharaoh Khufu (Cheops). By the beginning of the Christian era, though, the major shipbuilding center of the western world was in Genoa, Italy, and the nearby rivers were filled with logs floated down from the mountains. Shipbuilding was largely responsible for the disappearance of forests in the Mediterranean area.

For thousands of years wood has played a prominent role in warfare. From the time ancient man learned that he could club a foe with a tree branch, wood has figured in man's organized attempts to kill his fellow man. Spears, arrows, assault towers, war chariots, and battering rams were all made from wood. In older times, wood fueled the fires that heated the oil that protectors of castles poured on their enemies' heads. More recently, it fired the boilers of locomotives that pulled trains carrying soldiers and weapons to the Front. In World Wars I and II, the forests of the Near East took a terrible beating because of this.

Wood is used in the production of paper, of which Americans consume about 613 pounds per person each year. A modern paper-making machine can turn out seven hundred miles of newsprint or eleven hundred miles of toilet paper in one day. A run of the Sunday edition of the New York Times consumes the equivalent of seventy thousand trees eight inches in diameter.

Many chemicals come from wood or its byproducts. Tannin is obtained from the bark, leaves, and unripe fruit of several species of trees, and has been used to tan leather since ancient times. A synthetic product is used in commercial tanneries now, although some companies that make leather for specialized purposes still use natural

tannin. Turpentine and natural rubber come from trees.
An entire city rose in the Brazilian jungle financed on the
extraction, processing, and shipping of the sap of the
rubber tree, *Hivea brasiliensis*. And huge fortunes were
made by rubber barons who controlled the industry until
the demands of World War II forced the development of
synthetic rubber.

We owe a major debt to trees for many of the medicines
used today. Until synthetic medicine replaced quinine in
the 1940s, a chemical derived from the bark of a genus of
trees known as *Cinchona* was the only medication for
malaria. Its use went back three hundred years to the
eastern slopes of the Andes in Columbia and Bolivia.
Legends arose about the discovery of the material as a
medicine. In one of them, a cinchona tree was said to
have fallen into a pool of water, and the quinine leached
out. A malarial Indian supposedly drank from the pool
and was cured. In another legend, the Countess of
Chinchon is said to have been cured of malaria, thus
giving the tree its botanical name. In any event, when
Europeans learned about quinine, such a rush ensued
that the tree almost became extinct.

Today another tree could be in comparable danger.
Scientific experimentation has shown that a derivative of
the Pacific yew tree, taxol, is effective in treating certain
kinds of cancer. In the Pacific Northwest there has been a
rush by "pirates" to strip these trees of their bark. Because
the Pacific yew takes about eighty years to reach maturity,
unless very rigorous protection is enacted, this valuable
source of medicine could be in danger. (At this writing,
the synthetic production of taxol appears possible.)

There are probably many other medicines in the forest.
And unless we are careful to protect what is left of the
earth's forests, we might never find out, to our own
detriment.

In 1910, a few years before I was born, the U.S. Forest
Service established a research center in Madison,
Wisconsin, to study the uses we make of wood and wood

products, and to discover still others. The Forest Products Laboratory has been responsible for new food flavorings, adhesives, gasohol, improved wooden beams, and other construction materials.

So the question is not whether we will continue to need wood. We will. The real question is how we will manage the planet's forests. Thus far worldwide, we have done, and are doing, a very poor job of it. Worldwide, we cut and otherwise destroy far more forest than we replant. Seen just from the economic perspective, it doesn't make sense. We are destroying one of our most important natural resources as though there were no tomorrow.

A tree, acting as a windbreak, can save from ten percent to fifty percent of home heating costs in winter.

One tree can supply seventy-five dollars worth of soil erosion and storm water control each year.

Trees on one acre of land can release enough oxygen each day to fill the needs of eighteen people.

One tree can supply wildlife habitat worth seventy-five dollars per year.

Trees on your property can increase its market value up to fifteen percent.

A tree can absorb about thirteen pounds of carbon dioxide each year. An acre of trees can absorb up to two and one-half tons, roughly equivalent to the amount produced by driving a car twenty-six thousand miles.

Trees filter out between seventy and eighty-five percent of airborne particulates.

Chapter 3

In the fall of the year I was thirteen, our family left the hilltop farm in Polk County and moved onto a five-acre place a few miles southeast of Portland. Mary, Emily, Ralph, Victor, and I had never been to a large city before. (The largest we had seen was McMinnville, a tiny farming community west of Portland.) So coming to the city with its tall buildings was quite a thrill. My father pointed them out to me as we rode the inter-urban car line out to the Watson station near the tiny farm where we would live for several years. It's a wonder I didn't sunburn my tonsils, gawking up as I did. But then in the Northwest, that's hard to do. They say that we Oregonians don't tan; we rust.

It was quite an overwhelming experience changing from the Harmony school, which had maybe twenty children, to one with five or six hundred. I suppose we children from the country made many ridiculous social blunders at first.

Our place—in the little community of Lents—was about three blocks from the Portland General Electric tracks. At that time the company was building a dam up on the Clackamas River for hydroelectric generation, and used a narrow-gauge railroad to haul in supplies. In addition to carrying supplies in to the dam site, the railroad brought out logs from the mountains. I remember train after train loaded with logs rumbling past the house almost every fifteen or twenty minutes. The logs were chained on flat cars and brought to the Willamette River, where they were dumped in and lashed into rafts. The rafts were towed downriver to mills in Portland, or were disassembled, and the logs loaded on freighters that took them overseas.

Even in those long-gone days, many of the logs that came out of our mountains never saw the inside of an American mill! Now the railroad is abandoned. There's been no timber traffic on the upper Willamette for years. Most of the trees in that area have been cut down and are gone.

Although we had just five acres of land at Lents, we kept a couple of cows, I suppose for their milk. There was room for a garden and pasturage for the cows. And there was Johnson Creek.

Johnson Creek flowed along the back of our place. Upstream was the Southeast Portland Lumber Company, which impounded water from Johnson Creek to form their millpond, where logs were stored and sorted for the mill. Every few days, the dam gates were opened to allow water to flow out of the pond and down the creek.

The released water carried pieces of bark and wood along with it, so I rigged up a boom pole—a long pole set at an angle across the creek. Debris coming downstream hit the pole and was forced to our side of the creek. There I stood, on a small dock I'd built out into the stream. As the wood scraps came by, I'd flip them with a pitchfork onto the stream bank for use as firewood. It probably wasn't an especially good idea, since the dock was very flimsy and could have been swept away in the rush of released water. But we had plenty of firewood.

I also suspect I enjoyed seeing myself as an old-time white-water man. Although their day had long passed, they were still heroes to the boys growing up in logging country.

Not that we had any of them in the Northwest, even in the early days of logging. The white-water men worked in the woods of Maine and the other New England states. Their's was probably the most dangerous job in the woods. These were the men dressed in wool longjohns, "tin" pants, wool shirts, and heavy, studded boots called caulks (pronounced "corks") and carrying pike poles or peaveys. They stepped off good, solid dry land, onto logs floating down the rivers of New England, usually in springtime when the water was high and the drive was on. They kept the logs in the channel, free of the banks, and when there was a jam, the white-water men climbed out there to free the king log. If the jam went out with a rush, they stayed aboard, riding the logs all the way downstream to the millpond. Small wonder they became heroes to any boy growing up in timber country.

There were animals in Johnson Creek in those days—muskrats and mink mainly, no beaver. They had been trapped out more than one hundred years earlier by the mountain men.

They were a breed apart, those mountain men. Today we'd call them misanthropes. They were loners, staying ahead of civilization, even in colonial days. They were subsistence hunters and fishermen, and what cash they accrued, they derived from trapping. Early in the nineteenth century, beaver hats became the rage in Europe, and many fortunes in America were founded on the pelts of this industrious rodent. The town of Astoria, at the mouth of the Columbia, is named for its founder, John Jacob Astor, who established a trading post there early in the nineteenth century. The famed Astor fortune was built on beaver pelts.

Beaver trapping fit hand-in-glove with the mountain man's lifestyle. It took place in the wilderness, well away from the sounds and sights of civilization, and it could be conducted by a man living all by himself. It was a natural for these freedom-loving eccentrics.

But it was also a dead-end profession. By the time the beaver-hat craze was history, so were most of the beaver. The mountain men swept across the continent, cleaning out every reachable stream of its beaver population. When they reached Oregon they found a trapper's heaven—untold beaver streams, each loaded with the furry creatures. The trappers figured it could go on forever. But forty years after commercial trapping began in earnest, the beaver were gone, except for a few isolated families living on small streams in far-out corners of the territory.

The mountain men had crossed three thousand miles

of the continent to stay away from civilization. When they reached the Pacific, their backs were against the sea, and there was no place left to go. In just a few years, they slipped into history, much as the beaver they had trapped.

But their legends lived on, and every red-blooded country boy in the Northwest who didn't dream of white-water men adopted the rugged mountain man as a hero. Francis Bergendahl's brother, Jack, and I swaggered with the best of them. We decided that we were going to Alaska and maybe northern Canada to run trap lines when we grew up. We built a little cabin there by Johnson Creek, and nailed a crudely lettered sign over the door. CAMP KILLUM. We stocked the cabin with a few animal traps we'd found and some pieces of old guns and so forth.

My older brother Harold saw what we were up to and offered some advice. He helped us find a good site to set the traps, a shallow spot where we could slide them in the water, maybe an inch below the surface. He taught us how to camouflage the traps, so if any animals came along they wouldn't see the traps.

Jack and I followed Harold's instructions and trapped two beautiful mink. As I recall, we caught a couple of muskrats also. Harold helped us skin them and we shipped the pelts to Biggs Company in Kansas City, Missouri. In return, we received a check for $12.75, a lot of money back in 1925. Jack and I divided the money and each of us bought a pair of leather boots, really good boots.

Considering all the fooling around I did on Johnson Creek, it's a wonder I never fell in. And it's also a good thing that I didn't. I couldn't swim a stroke. A few years later, when I was in the Boy Scouts, my lifelong friend, Allan de Lay, taught me to swim.

One time Johnson Creek came one rock short of becoming a battleground. There were a couple of gangs of boys in Lents, and they made a career of not liking each other. These weren't what we think of as gangs today. They didn't use drugs; we had never heard of drugs. They didn't drink, and most of them didn't smoke. They were just boys who liked to swagger around, flexing their muscles and spitting a lot. One of the ways they tried to prove how tough they were was by fighting.

The leader of one of the gangs was Francis Bergendahl. He lived across the road from our place. Francis was... well, I'd say he was kind of tough. He was the most respected boy in school. He was a good fighter and could lick most everybody. He was also smart, so the ones he couldn't lick he bribed. He was kind of like an eight-hundred-pound gorilla; he did just about anything he wanted.

Francis and his gang figured they were the toughest boys in Lents. But there was another gang with the same idea. The two of them decided to fight it out. Not with guns—we never heard of such a thing—but with slingshots. These slingshots were made of a crotch from a small tree, a couple of pieces of rubber cut out of an old inner tube, and a leather pouch. You put a rock in the pouch, pinched it between a forefinger and your thumb, pulled back as far as you could, and let her fly. If that rock hit somebody in the eye, it could cause a lot of damage, but usually it missed altogether.

The coming battle was the talk of all the kids, who argued about who would beat whom. The odds favored Francis. The two gangs got in the spirit and decided to make the event a really big thing. They agreed to have the battle across Johnson Creek. Francis' group would position themselves on our side, and the other gang would come downstream from Indian Rock on the other side of the creek. They would fight it out across the stream. I don't know how I got out of being pressed into service by Francis, but I did.

Somehow my father got wind of the big war and when the kids began to assemble, he walked out and told them to "git" or he would call the sheriff. That was the end of the biggest social event of the year. I always suspected the combatants were just as happy that a Higher Authority had stepped in.

Francis Bergendahl could be a little bit mean in his

methods of persuasion. I remember one occasion when I went up with him on Mt. Scott. There was a boy up there by himself, just a little kid, maybe nine or ten years old. Francis said, "Let's capture him," and pushed the boy into a small circle he had scratched in the dirt. Francis told him not to move or he would shoot him with the slingshot. I don't think he would have, but the boy started to cry and Francis relented and let him go.

One of the boys who belonged to Francis' gang had a Model T Ford or some old car. We were driving around in the Mt. Scott area near home on a back road where farmers kept their beehives for winter. (In winter the bees have to have the honey they made in the summer or they will starve.) The boys pulled up by the farmer's place where the hives were sitting out in the field. One of the boys ran out and took the top off one of the hives, grabbed a cone of honey and ran back to the car, where everybody had some of it.

The honey was pretty sweet and good, but I knew it was wrong to do that. If bees are well fed and have plenty of honey to eat during winter, they can generate enough warmth to survive. But bees will not come out of the hive in cool weather. They can't function when the temperature is below fifty-five degrees.

When we moved to Lents, I was first placed in a class that I suppose you could say wasn't one of the best in the school. The kids were tough, like Francis Bergendahl, and not much interested in learning or otherwise bettering themselves. I guess I told my dad about it. Anyway, he visited the principal, and I was transferred into another class where the kids were more friendly and a lot of them belonged to the Boy Scouts of America.

About that same time, Francis Bergendahl got a part-time job as the foreman of sorts for a crew of boys who delivered handbills for the local theater, the Yeager. He asked me to work for him. Our pay was a dozen tickets each month to the theater, which allowed our family to go to a movie once in a while. The Woodmere Scout Troop 104 was going to put on a fund-raiser show at the

Yeager. Francis and I were assigned to be the Scouts' bosses
when they delivered handbills advertising the show.

Although I was interested in the Scouts, I didn't want
to join because the kids in that first class I had been in
considered them sissies and pantywaists. Francis called
them "bottle suckers."

I wasn't about to be a bottle sucker.

But the more the Scouts told me about their activities,
the more interested I became. Finally I sneaked off to a
meeting, and after that, I never missed another one. I
sneaked because I didn't want my parents to know I was
associated with that sissy bunch. But when they found
out, rather than scolding me, they thought it was such a
good idea they prevailed on my brother Ralph to go along.
The two of us became Boy Scouts, and later on, our brother
Victor joined.

Troop 104 held its meetings outdoors around a
campfire. The very first night I attended, the Patrol Leader,
Bill Fague, passed me on my Tenderfoot requirements. I
couldn't figure that out. I didn't even know what the
requirements were. I hadn't studied the handbook, in
fact, I didn't have one. But Bill passed me. Many years
later, he told me why. "Frank, you had a reputation around
school as a tough guy, because you hung out with Francis
Bergendahl. I figured you'd beat me up if I didn't pass you."

I doubt Francis ever realized how responsible he was for
my starting a Boy Scout career on such a successful note.

From that first meeting, I was totally committed to the
Boy Scouts. They were involved in the very things that
were important in my life—nature, the forests, learning
how to take care of oneself in the woods, good citizenship,
character building. And since that first meeting, I have
been a registered Scout continuously for sixty-eight years,
and have served in many capacities.

Troop 104 was located in a poor section of Portland,
and most of the families had very little money, hardly
enough to outfit their sons with Boy Scout uniforms and
equipment. Much to our delight, the company that
manufactured the uniforms announced a contest to

demonstrate how sturdy their trousers were, and offered free trousers to teams of six boys who could tear them. Our boys showed up and ripped open those new pants, crotch to bottom, as though they were made of tissue paper!

Then a competing company held the same contest with their trousers. Our team from Troop 104 did it again. All the boys in the troop who couldn't afford that essential part of the Scout uniform got free pants.

After I had been in the troop a few years, a small group of the older boys decided to go into the woods on a two-week hike. There would be no adult leadership, just us. We'd hike, fish, view the scenery, and have a good time. The food for feeding these eight or nine boys for two weeks came to sixteen dollars. We planned every step of the way, so by the time we hitchhiked out to the trailhead, we were confident that every possible contingency was accounted for.

Except for rain.

You'd think that Boy Scouts living in Oregon would understand it can rain any day of the year up here. But with the arrogance—and thoughtlessness—of youth, we ignored it.

In those times before the Civilian Conservation Corps (CCC) had built hundreds of miles of trails in Oregon's forests, most trails were marked simply by blazes, a bit of bark chopped off the trees. A person made his way by hiking from one blaze mark to the next.

Aside from the rain, the first part of the trip went well. The fishermen in the group were happy. The mountain climbers had plenty of peaks—the entire Cascade range is made up of volcanic peaks. And the goof-offs had plenty of time to lie around.

About half through the trip, trouble hit. Three of the boys decided we were lost, and took off by themselves. Two of them were discovered by a trail-building crew who put them up for the better part of a week. The third boy wandered around for a few days, then finally straggled into a ranger station. Nobody was actually hurt, but the experience taught me a lesson. I was supposed to be the leader of the expedition, yet had allowed it all to happen. From that point on, whenever I have been in charge, I take charge. If mistakes are made, they are my mistakes and I'll answer for them. That lesson has served me well. (All the boys who went along on the hike have remained good friends to this day.)

A few years after I joined the troop, Floyd W. Allen, a civil engineer in Portland, volunteered to organize a group of older Scouts into an engineering unit. Several of us from Troop 104 took advantage of this and joined up. The unit was divided into corps, and eventually I became the leader of one of them. One of our first projects was to survey and map a Scout camp outside of Portland. Camp Millard had been given to the Council several years earlier and was a favorite campsite for many of the troops, in large measure because of its accessibility. Millard was big, 350 acres or so, and criss-crossed by creeks, washouts and hills. It was a great place to learn surveying. We learned all the basic procedures—use of the transit, working on the chain gang, and so forth. When we were finished, the Council had an accurate topographical map of its most popular camp.

Another project the Engineers undertook was to design and build a bridge to span a creek at Camp Millard. It was two hundred feet long and portable, at least in the beginning. After we had done all the engineering and basic construction, we disassembled the bridge and took it to a Scout rally, where we put it back together in just thirty minutes. After the rally, the bridge was taken out to Camp Millard and permanently assembled. The engineering unit lasted for three or four years. It was a good training program and proved valuable to some of the boys when they went into military service during the war.

Years later, when the Boy Scout organization established the Explorer program for older boys and girls, its programs were very much like that Mr. Allen had developed for his engineering unit in Portland.

Camp Millard was a great place for the Scouts to work on their merit badges. These badges are given to boys who master certain skills and form the prerequisites for advancement to certain ranks. There are 124 of them in subjects ranging from agriculture to wood working. Each Scout is encouraged to earn merit badges, and camp is an excellent place to work on many of them. The work I did earning certain badges such as forestry, agriculture, soil management and other outdoor skills did much to raise my interest and involvement in forest practices, and especially the replanting of idle lands with forest trees. I must admit, though, that one or two gave me some trouble. For example, the Lifesaving merit badge is a requirement for a person to become an Eagle Scout, the highest rank, and I didn't know how to swim. My friend, Allan de Lay, an expert swimmer and diver, helped me. I'd never have passed that Lifesaving test if it hadn't have been for Allan. He went on to become a world-class diver, and in his later years has won contests in the Masters Division.

One of the challenges Scouting has faced over the years has been to retain older youth whose interests do not necessarily coincide with those of younger boys. That's why we formed the Engineers. It was obvious that something comparable would be included in the Boy Scouts' national Explorer program. After the program came into being, I organized ten Forestry Explorer Posts and an Engineering Post in just one year. An important part of their program has been planting trees.

In 1977, as Membership Chairman of the Associated General Contractors, I thought it might be a good idea for the association to sponsor an engineering Explorer Post for high school boys and girls who were interested in engineering and contracting. The association bought the idea. I approached an old friend, Ralph Hannan, a contractor who had been a Scout in Troop 104 way back when. He agreed to be the Post Advisor, a position comparable to the Scoutmaster's job in the Boy Scouts. Explorer Post 869 became an outstanding organization and is still going strong, although Ralph hung up the Advisor job after seventeen years.

A few years ago, Ralph's Post built a bridge at Butte Creek Boy Scout Ranch, over a large stream that flows through the camp. In springtime, this stream can be awesome. Ralph scrounged two steel trusses from an abandoned bridge someplace, and the Post trucked them to Butte Creek one February day. The move wasn't easy. The trusses were about seventy feet long, and the road into the ranch was narrow and twisting. At one point, the Explorers had to lower a power line to get the trusses around a curve. It was like trying to shove a size-twelve foot into a size-ten shoe. By spring the bridge was completed. I went out to see it with Ralph and he showed me a plaque his Explorers had mounted at one end. They had named their structure the Frank H. Lockyear Bridge. I can't figure out why the Explorers did that, but I feel honored, nonetheless. Ralph told me that, at that time, there was only one other bridge named for someone still living. Since then the other person has died, so I have the honor all to myself.

The outdoors has always been important in Scouting, and those of us living in the Northwest are blessed to have so much of it. The Cascade Mountains, literally at our back door, offer millions of acres of forests, lakes, rivers, and peaks. Mt. Hood, just forty miles east of Portland, is one of the most perfect peaks in the area. At 11,235 feet above sea level, it is the highest point in the state. Next to Fujiyama, it is the most climbed peak in the world. The various routes up it have something for everybody, from rank amateurs to world-class climbers. In 1933 the Columbia Pacific Scout Council arranged a climb for Eagle Scouts from the Portland area. I think about twenty-five boys signed up, including a couple of us from Troop 104. In those days, a climb of Mt. Hood began at about four thousand feet elevation in the village of Government Camp. Now climbers leave from the Timberline Lodge, six thousand feet above sea level, or even take a snow cat to the top of Palmer glacier at eight thousand feet.

The Eagle Scout climb was held early in May, a time

when the weather can change drastically and fast in the Northwest. The day was blustery as I recall, the kind of day when we probably shouldn't have made the climb, I suppose. But we did. Out of those twenty-five Scouts, only five of us reached the summit: Allan de Lay and I, plus three of our friends from other troops. The others dropped out and wandered back to the starting point.

About six months after I joined Troop 104, we got a new Scoutmaster, Fred York, who would be our leader for the next twenty-seven years. Even though I was just a kid of fourteen, he put me in charge of organizing the Troop's tree plantings and its other activities. We planted thousands of trees in those years.

When I was nineteen years old, or thereabouts, I was invited to be the assistant to our Sunrise District Commissioner. This was quite an honor for so young a person. Within a short time, the District Commissioner resigned, and I was appointed District Commissioner for Sunset District, Columbia-Pacific Council. Of course, it was a volunteer position, paying no salary, so I had to squeeze it in with my regular work. My responsibilities included making sure the troops in the District were fully registered on time each year, and recruiting new troops. After being on the job for a while, I was summoned to the Council headquarters in downtown Portland. The Scout Executive in those days was an energetic man named George Herman Oberteuffer. Everybody called him Obie. When I arrived at his office, he told me that I had been appointed to a special recruiting committee in company with a local millionaire, another of Portland's movers and shakers, and the local Roman Catholic bishop, plus Obie himself. He looked me in the eye and said, "By the committee's next meeting, you'd better bring in some new troops."

Here I was, practically no more than a kid, working alongside those important people. I figured I'd better get moving.

I chose a school and contacted the principal. I explained that I was associated with the Boy Scouts and asked if I could meet with all the boys twelve years and older who were not already Scouts. He was very cooperative. "Mr. Lockyear, I'll have the boys in such and such a room in twenty minutes." Well, about fifteen kids showed up, clean-cut, nice boys. I explained who I was and why I was there, showed them my Scout uniform, told them what we did in the Scouts—camping, seeing wild animals, learning things, advancing in rank, and so on. I invited them to a meeting at that school at seven in the evening. When they left, I asked the principal for the use of a room. He agreed, and we were in business. I asked my brother, Ralph, and a friend, Hilding Foleen, both Eagle Scouts, to handle this new troop. I recruited local citizens to serve on the troop committee, and Troop 66 came into being. It was in existence for fifty years.

I also organized Troop 30, led initially by my good friend, Allan de Lay, and it still exists, sixty years later. I organized Troop 108, and quite a few others, including one in Wilsonville, Oregon, when I moved here. I am still a member of that troop's committee.

I always enjoyed school, even Harmony school with its one room. When we came into town, with its larger schools, I became even more interested. I was what might be called a diligent student. I recall one time when I was in the eighth grade, ready to move on to high school, and Louis Reghitto and I were playing handball and collided on the court. I fell, breaking a collarbone. I ran to a doctor's office and had the injury immobilized. I insisted on returning to school because there was a special award for eighth-grade students who had perfect attendance, and I really wanted it. So, broken collarbone and all, I stayed in school. A couple of weeks after the accident, one of our neighbors, Bernie Kearns, who had a small truck garden, asked me to do some cultivating for him. I mentioned my broken bone, but he just said that a good, strong country boy such as I was should be able to handle the matter. I couldn't use my right arm, so I had to control the horse with only my left hand. He hitched up the horse and I gave it a try. But I didn't do much of a job for Bernie, and he never paid me.

My brothers and I worked for several truck gardeners in the area. One of our favorite bosses was Sam Fuji, the old uncle who ran the farm for the rest of his family. He went out in the field to work alongside us, teaching us the best methods. Then after working for a hour or so, he'd say, "Come on, boys. Let's go sit down." We'd go rest for a few minutes, and another member of the family would bring out cookies or pop or a piece of watermelon.

Another Japanese family asked my brother Ralph and me to work for them after we were done with the Fuji's. This family had a pack of dogs, one of which seemed to have a dislike for me. He'd come dashing out, baring his teeth as if he were going to tear my leg off. I always carried something like a rake with which to protect myself. Mrs. Imazzu, who ran the farm, didn't like that, I guess, because she came out and pointed at me. "You we no like," she said. "We like Ralpha, but you go home." So that was the end of my work at the Imazzu farm. Ralph worked for them for several years, and ending up making $2.50 a day, which was a lot of money in those Depression days.

After living in Lents for several years, my father moved the family to Portland proper, into an area called Sellwood. The cows went along with us, but there was no land for grazing, so we staked them out in the park across the street, then put them in the basement at night. That arrangement didn't stand a chance. Soon we got rid of the cows, and that was our last experience with farm animals.

I started high school after we moved to Sellwood. Right off the bat I was elected president of the freshman class. (One of my friends was the official ballot counter.)

Gym was a required class, and each boy was expected to have a proper gym suit. But in 1927 or '28, poor families like ours couldn't afford any extras, and exercise clothes were definitely an extra. So all I had to wear to the class was my longjohn underwear. I guess I was quite a sight, but what could I do? The teacher, Mr. Carr, wasn't amused. His method of keeping control of the class was to run the guilty boy through what he called "The Paddle Mill." This was a group of older gym boys with big, wide paddles who formed a gauntlet through which we had to run, getting whacked all the way. After this happened to me a couple of times, I simply didn't go back to gym class. The Vice Principal, Colton Meek, then called me to his office, and asked why I was skipping a class. "You are an outstanding freshman. You have been elected president, and are supposed to be an example for your whole class, and here you are not doing your duty." I didn't tell him why I was such a poor example. I simply left school. I had been there just a few weeks, and I never went back.

Chapter 4

I started looking for a job right away, but there were precious few of them. The country was headed into the Great Depression, and there were family men lined up to get anything that would put food on the table. What chance did a kid with practically no experience have? But I was young and strong and optimistic.

My mother made a lunch for me each morning and I would walk up and down streets, stopping in businesses, willing to take anything that would make a few dollars. I even went down to Portland's waterfront, hoping to get a berth on some merchant vessel. One day a longshoreman stopped me and we started talking. He told me to follow him, and I thought I was to be given a job. But he took me under a pier and tried to take down my pants. I fought him off and ran. He tried to catch me. I guess he figured I was going to call the police, but all I wanted was to get out of there.

Finally, after a couple of months, I found a job in a tannery not too far from home. The place was wet and it stank, but I made twenty-five cents an hour and liked the work. It was kind of interesting to handle the hides that came in and turn them into leather. After a couple of months, I asked the boss for a raise. I figured I was worth more than two bits an hour. But the boss was not keen about offering me a future with the company. He just said that when I learned how to do things without being told, he would consider giving me the raise. That wasn't quite enough for me. That Saturday I asked for my pay and never went back. I was back pounding the pavement.

Two of my sisters were working at Jantzen Knitting

Mills, which made the famous swimwear. They told me the mill was hiring, so I went down there and stood in line. I was called in to be interviewed by the person in charge of hiring, Mr. Carl Vreeland. He asked how old I was. I was honest and said fifteen. He asked about my schooling. I fibbed. I said I had attended for a couple of years and got good grades in all subjects except Latin. Mr. Vreeland nodded and said he had not done well in Latin either. He went on to say that much as he would like to hire me, state law required that a person be at least eighteen.

I went home and told my mother. She was a very moral and ethical person who didn't believe in lying and so on. But she said, "I don't think it will harm your character or spirit if you tell a falsehood about your age in order to get a job." I didn't tell her about all that stuff about my grades in high school. No point in pushing my luck. A couple of weeks later I went back to Jantzen and stood in line again. This time I was interviewed by a different person, and I told him I was eighteen and had two years of high school. He hired me on the spot and told me to report that evening to work on the swing shift—seven-thirty in the evening until two-thirty in the morning.

I was assigned to the winding department, working on machines that rewound yarn to check its strength before it went through the knitting machines. If we found a break, we were to stop the machine and tie the yarn with a special knot they taught us. I never did do too well in the winding department. The boss scolded me several times. He would come up behind me and say, "Young fellow, you've got to do better." But he was generally nice. One day he came up, slapped me on the back and said, "You come with me," and marched me through the building over to another department. I figured this was it. But in the other department I met a really nice person, Alex Masson, who headed the yarn supply department. My old boss laughed and said, "Frank, I've got you another job over here." He thought that was quite a joke, to march me over as though he were going to fire me. I did well in this new department, but when the Depression really hit I got laid off with the understanding that I would be called back when things picked up. This happened a few times over the next two or three years, and eventually I figured I needed a steady job.

But in 1932 the country was in the depths of the Great Depression, and there were few jobs to be had. I contacted all the people I knew, including a man I had worked with in the tannery. He had his own company by then and said that I could work for him at a dollar a day. I left home on a Monday morning and started walking—it was five miles to the tannery. I cut cross-country and got to the corner of 28th Street and Steele, where there was a wide board walkway alongside the street. Several men were planting attractive little trees along it. I walked over and watched them for a couple of minutes.

There has always seemed something almost magical to me about a tree being planted. It's like a new birth. Here is this little stick of a thing, maybe bare root or with the roots balled in burlap. It's put into the rich earth. Soil is carefully packed around it. A gallon or so of water is poured at the base, almost like a blessing. Then slowly it begins to grope through the ground for nutrients and moisture. Leaves appear on the twigs. I get the feeling that the little tree is beginning to find its place, that its spirit is finding its home. That little snip of a thing that was planted in the soil can become one of the most majestic things that God ever put on earth. It might soar up to three hundred feet into the sky. Its roots might probe one hundred feet into the soil. Its branches can spread fifty, sixty feet. It can eventually weigh many tons. It can live for centuries, seeing generation after generation of humanity come and go. It is almost immortal. Tell me, what more noble thing exists?

So I stood there in the street on that day so long ago, watching the workmen plant those little trees. One of the men asked, "Are you looking for a job?" I said that I was and he said, "Walk on down the sidewalk to the office and ask for Mr. Lambert."

The man who answered my knock on the office door was roughly fifty years old and dressed to the nines in a dark suit, white shirt, tie, and polished shoes. He had thick, black hair, and spoke in a soft, Georgian accent. I said that I was applying for work.

"What have you been doing?" Mr. Lambert asked.

"Digging ditches." Unlike the fictional high school grades and age I had given when I applied at Jantzens, this statement was true. I had been digging ditches for the local water district as a way of paying the family's water bill.

"Let me see your hands," Mr. Lambert snapped.

I held them out, palms up. They were rough and calloused, and there was dirt under the nails.

Mr. Lambert studied them for a moment, then said, "Come with me." I followed him from the office and down the wooden walk to a shed. "Bill!" Mr. Lambert called through the door. "Give this man a shovel."

That is how I began a job that would lead me to a way of life that continues to this day. Mr. Lambert was the founder of Lambert Gardens, which became one of Portland's outstanding and most famous visitor attractions.

I was put to work in the growing area. Mr. Lambert expected everybody to work hard and earn their dollar a day. At the beginning, that's what I got, one dollar a day. The work was hard, really hard; sometimes I didn't think I could get through the day. But each day was also a new adventure, as we moved around the city to new projects, and I felt good to have a part in all this. I enjoyed every minute of it, even the digging.

I tried to identify the different layers of topsoil as I dug through them, and got pretty good at it.

At Lambert Gardens, I started out root pruning trees. The purpose of root pruning is to prepare a tree for moving. It is done in late fall or winter when the tree is dormant—if it is deciduous—or when it isn't growing, in the case of evergreens. You begin a root pruning by digging a trench around the tree at a designated distance from the trunk, making sure to chop off all the roots. If the tree is going to be boxed, you make the trench square. If it's going to be balled, you make the trench circular. The tools you use are a sharp shovel, snips, and a saw to cut the roots cleanly. It's important that the roots not be mangled or smashed because they might decay. This can be dangerous to the tree's health. After the trench is about two feet deep, you start digging under the tree toward the center, cutting roots as you go. When the tree is free of the surrounding soil, it is tipped over to make sure all the roots are trimmed off neatly. Mr. Lambert insisted that we never leave roots hanging. The tree is then straightened and the hole backfilled with soil that is tamped firmly. The tree is immediately watered to make sure the earth is well-compacted. Properly done, root pruning frees the tree from the surrounding soil in a way that keeps it healthy, yet allows it to be boxed or balled. It stunts the tree but doesn't kill it, because the massive roots are not being cut when the tree is in full foliage. After root pruning, a tree can be moved just about any time of year.

I helped move some very large trees at Lambert's. Some were up to one foot in diameter, which is a pretty big tree to be moved. The really large ones were boxed rather than balled. In those days, we didn't have the big cranes that are used now. We would build a box around the tree, then cut under and build a bottom to the box. We put skids under the box and used a winch to pull the tree from the hole, moving it on large rollers up a ramp onto a truck or trailer for moving.

When the trees reached their new home, we rolled them down a ramp we had prepared into a hole. Or we would fasten the tree to an anchor on the other side of the hole, then drive out from under the box, letting the tree slide into the hole. It would take one or two weeks from the time we started digging the tree until it was finally in place in its new home.

Eventually I advanced from the root pruning gang into the Gardens' propagating house. Here thousands of cuttings were taken from different kinds of shrubs and trees, and potted. One of the species we rooted was western red cedar. They were nice cuttings and did well. One day in 1933, Mr. Lambert came through and told the propagator that most of the cedar should be destroyed because the Garden had too many of them. He ordered that five hundred be put on the burn pile.

Those little trees looked so nice, I couldn't even think of them being destroyed. I said, "Mr. Lambert, can I have these little trees?"

"No, Frank. I know why you want them. You'll get yourself a piece of land and start your own nursery and compete with me."

But I still couldn't accept the idea of those little trees being burned. On my day off, I visited the supervisor of Mt. Hood National Forest and told him my story. I asked if there might be a site in the forest where I could plant the little cedars where even Mr. Lambert couldn't accuse me of trying to compete with him. I said that in this case, Mr. Lambert might let me have them. The supervisor said he thought there might be such a place. He assigned one of his foresters, a Mr. Fullington, to help us. We went up the Clackamas River to a little place that seemed just right.

Back at the Gardens, I approached Mr. Lambert again. This time I told him what I planned to do: get a group of Boy Scouts together and go up the Clackamas to plant the cedar seedlings on Forest Service land. I told him there probably would be some publicity for Lambert Gardens in the deal. That turned the trick. He said to go ahead and take the cedar seedlings. I got about thirty-five Boy Scouts from around the District and we went out and planted those little western red cedars. That was in 1934. My friend, the photographer Allan de Lay, took motion pictures of the event. Later, during the war, fires in the area destroyed a few of the trees. But in 1988 or thereabout, the Mt. Hood National Forest historian, Tom Orlman, and I went to look for those that survived. Allan de Lay went along. We found some cedars that were of the right age and in the right place, so we figured that some of those original five hundred seedlings had survived through the years.

In addition to selling plants to the people who visited the Gardens, Mr. Lambert had a landscaping business. He was an expert in designing and installing beautiful gardens. Even during those Depression days, he was always busy, for there was a lot of wealth in Portland. I worked on crews that landscaped many of the best homes in the city, including that of the Jantzen Knitting Mills family. This home was built on an island in the middle of a lake that had been formed by diverting part of the flow of the Clackamas River. We hauled huge cedars out there. When Mr. Lambert needed such trees, and he didn't have them growing in his facility, he would scout the area, and when he found what he wanted, would negotiate with the owner. I remember digging, boxing and hauling huge trees from miles away just to satisfy Mr. Lambert's aesthetic sense of what a particular job should include. He had pretty firm ideas on how to design landscaping, and he usually convinced the owners. But when the bills came in, the owners were candidates for heart attacks.

In late autumn of 1936, Mr. Lambert got a large landscaping project at Courrier's Rancho, a resort at Lakeside, Oregon. It was so extensive it required two or three railroad cars of materials—fertilizer, peat moss, trees, shrubs, and so forth—to be shipped down there from Portland. Mr. Lambert chose me to run the job and sent along a couple of helpers. We were to live down there for the several months the project would take.

One day, the coldest day of the year, the rope on the property flagpole got tangled at the top. Mr. Lambert was down from Portland seeing how the job was going, and he and Mr. Courrier noticed the rope. Mr. Lambert called me over and said, "Frank, you climb up that pole and free the rope." I put on climbing spurs, and started up. (I'd never used climbing spurs before.) The pole had been barked and the wood was very hard, so I couldn't set the spurs and had to fight to stay on the pole, let alone climb. Eventually I reached the top and untangled the rope. But as I was starting down, Mr. Lambert yelled for me to paint the pole. He sent up a brush and a can of black paint. When I finally reached the ground, my hands, face and clothes were black. However, Mr. Courrier gave me ten dollars and said, "Here Frank, go get yourself some new clothes." In those days, that was a lot of money, enough to outfit me completely. Mr. Lambert never even thanked me for hanging on that pole in the cold.

We didn't get to finish the Courrier's Rancho project. While we were there, Mr. Courrier fell in love with his secretary who lived there with her husband. The two of them decamped for New York, leaving Mrs. Courrier to manage. The landscaping project fell through, and we returned home to Portland. I never learned how the romance turned out.

After I had a few years' experience moving big trees, leading landscaping jobs, and working in the propagating house and greenhouse, Mr. Lambert decided that he wanted me to help with sales. First I worked in the sales garden, waiting on people and carrying out the goods they bought. Later I was promoted to greet people as they came to the Gardens, escort them around, and if possible, help them choose plants. This meant becoming even more familiar with our plants, and I spent many hours bent over Bailey's Encyclopedia, learning about habitat and what grew where. We didn't want to recommend plants that wouldn't grow or do well in a customer's home area. The job became exciting to me. I met people from all around the world and had the chance to escort them through those beautiful gardens, explaining about the many trees and bushes growing there. Of course I didn't realize it, but this experience would prove very helpful to me later on as I began to do tree planting worldwide.

One spring day as I was escorting a small party of ladies around the Gardens, one of them who seemed to be the leader became quite excited about the plants, especially the rhododendrons and certain other perennials. She asked if we shipped and I answered that of course we did. She chose a large number of plants without even asking prices, and we arranged to ship them collect. This was a standard practice because, until we dug and balled the plants, we had no way of knowing how much they would weigh. The lady said this would be fine and gave me her name and address. She was Mrs. Alfred P. Sloane, wife of the president of General Motors. Mr. Lambert was not very happy with me when he found out I had sold to such a rich person. "Why Frank, I could have sold her thousands of dollars worth of material, and you got by with a few hundred. You need to sell fast and hard. People aren't going to be here in the Gardens very long and you have to get them right away."

Well, that wasn't my way of doing business, and I still ended up the best salesman at the Gardens. Mr. Lambert's son who was brought in from Georgia, was supposed to be a superb salesman but I made many times the sales he did. I think the main reason was that I didn't push. I would let people become acquainted with the Gardens, and would show them the lovely plants, especially those that would grow in their home regions. Eventually I would say that we did ship, and from then on it was simply a matter of writing down the orders.

Another time, a little girl came to the Gardens with two adults, a man and woman. I took them around and they seemed very impressed, and remarked that the girl's mother, Mrs. MacArthur, surely would enjoy this and that she must come the following day. Sure enough, the next day a lovely lady and her husband showed up. They were especially interested in our tulips. Mr. Lambert always had the finest bulbs shipped in from Holland for springtime showing of the blooms. The man and lady stopped at several of the most outstanding beds, and I picked a blossom and gave it to her. She thanked me and said that I needn't stay with them. I pretended not to hear, and kept walking along, explaining about this and that. Gradually she began asking about the plants. I answered, never suggesting that she buy, and finally she asked if we shipped. She ended up buying a large selection of plants, and that is how I came to meet Helen Hayes. I learned later that her daughter, the little girl I had met the day before, died not many years later.

By 1939, I was married and my wife had a baby on the way. That winter I stayed home a couple of times to help her. That was unusual for me, since I worked seven days a week at Lambert Gardens. I put in long hours, upwards of eleven each day in summer. You could say I kept my nose to the grindstone. But when I took a couple of days off, it bothered Mr. Lambert. Maybe he thought I was taking advantage of him. A day or so later, he called me into the office and said, "Frank, I'm going to give you a chance to make a lot of money. Starting next month you are on straight commission. You will get twenty percent of everything you sell. The sky's the limit and you can go as fast and far as you want."

I said, "Well, Mr. Lambert, next month happens to be the worst month of the year for the Gardens. So I don't think that's much of an opportunity."

"Well anyway, starting next month we're going to do it," he said. "I'll give you seventy-five dollars a month on a drawing account."

"Well, Mr. Lambert, I don't think so. I'm leaving here right now and I'm not coming back."

I had been with him for seven years, and had done a good job from the moment I started. I figured this commission business was his way of getting me to work even harder than I was. Although I saw him after that and even helped him out a couple of times when I had my own business, I never did go back. Lambert Gardens closed in 1968, and Mr. Lambert died in 1974 at the age of eighty-eight.

Technically, soil is the loose, weathered, mineral and organic debris that lies over the subsoil. The organic part is called humus and is made up of leaves, grasses, twigs, rotting trees, algae and fungi, bacteria, animal droppings, and even the decomposing bodies of the animals themselves. The kinds of soil are largely determined by climate, the underlying minerals, topography, and how long the soil has been forming. Mineral and organic material might make up less than one-half of the soil's overall volume, the rest of the space being taken up by air and water.

Mature soil needs to remain undisturbed for at least ten thousand years to develop. When the natural cover, such as grass or trees, is stripped away, water, frost, wind, and gravity can erode living soil away in less than fifty years.

About ten thousand years ago, humanity discovered a more reliable and plentiful supply of food in growing crops and herding animals than in hunting and food gathering. But these crops and the pastures needed for the animals depended on fertile soil. So soil can be said to have been largely responsible for the development of civilization. But even before humans developed farming and pastoralism, they depended on good soil, for it was this that produced the grasses for game animals and the cereals, tubers, nuts, and berries that people gathered.

Today we are seeing a tragic loss of soil through poor farming methods, overgrazing, fire, and deforestation. The more industrialized countries make some effort to take care of their soil. In the United States, for example, more than fifteen billion dollars have been spent in the last fifty years on various soil conservation methods. But in the developing countries, all too often the story is one of soil erosion caused by poverty, inequality, and poor agricultural methods, leading to drought, desertification, floods, and famine. Right now, as I write this, Somalia is suffering a drought and famine, caused at least, in part, by the destruction of the soil.

Probably the worst example in the Western Hemisphere of what can happen from unwise use of the soil is found in Haiti. When Columbus first landed in the New World, he noted the heavy, lush forests that covered the island of Santo Domingo, the island on which Haiti is located. Today there are practically no forests left. In fact the hillsides are stripped of all vegetation, and the soil has largely been washed into the sea.

But the destruction certainly isn't restricted to that one, poverty-stricken country. About ten percent of

Ethiopia's cropland is lost to erosion annually, a loss of about seventeen tons per acre per year. And Nepal, in the Himalayas, loses more than one and one-half *billion* tons of its soil per year. The United Nations' Food and Agriculture Organization estimates that, worldwide, almost three million acres of productive land (soil) is lost to erosion each year.

Chapter 5

The size and vigor of a tree is determined not only by its species, but the environmental conditions in which it grows. For example, a quaking aspen might grow to be one hundred feet tall in the lower elevations of the species' range. But a quaking aspen growing high in the mountains will be lucky to exceed four or five feet. Willow that grow to six feet or more in the lower latitudes will crawl along the tundra in the Arctic.

Wind shapes trees. The Monterey cypress that grows along the northern California coast is sculpted by the prevailing winds that come in from the west, giving the trees a lopsided look. A few miles from my home in Oregon, there is an area which gets frequent and intense dosages of a wind blowing from the east. The trees that grow here, especially the Douglas fir, have the eastern sides of their top few feet pretty well stripped of branches. But just a few miles away, outside the windy area, the firs are perfectly round and conical.

Moisture and soil have a marked effect on the growth of trees. The bristlecone pine of the desert mountains in the American southwest is noted for not only its extreme age, but for its twisted, stunted appearance. This occurs in trees that grow in the poor soil of moisture-starved mountains. The same species, growing a few hundred feet lower, are much taller and more fully foliaged.

Earth has had trees for more then three hundred million years, from the Carboniferous and Devonian periods. Today's coal existed as Carboniferous forests, which covered just about all the land areas of the earth. There are still a couple of survivors of very early tree forms. The metasequoia, also called the dawn redwood, is a very old species. It was discovered still growing in the interior of China in 1948. And there are certain cycads left, the remnants of another ancient group of trees.

Trees are classified in two basic groups, gymnosperms and angiosperms. Gymnosperms are the older of the two, and are characterized by seeds not enclosed in an ovary, thus their name: Gymno, which means naked, and sperm, which means seed. The second group of trees, the angiosperms, are characterized as having seeds that are enclosed in an ovary; angio means vessel or cover. Angiosperms first appeared about 160 million years ago.

The best known and most numerous of the gymnosperms are the conifers—pines, fir, spruce, cedar, hemlock, of which there are more than four hundred species. A conifer is characterized by a woody cone in which the seeds are produced. Most conifers have needles instead of broad leaves, and usually stay green year-round. One exception to this is the larch, which drops all its needles much as a deciduous tree sheds its leaves. Larch usually grow among other species, such as Douglas fir and hemlock, in the western mountains. In autumn, the brilliant yellow of their foliage seen against the dark, almost black green of the other trees, is quite beautiful.

The conifers, like all angiosperms, are called softwood trees, although in some cases they produce lumber that is much harder than that of some of the hardwood species.

Hardwoods are the broadleafed trees—oaks, elms, maples, birch, as well as more than one thousand other species. Those growing in the temperate zones are deciduous, shedding their leaves at the end of the growing season. Tropical hardwoods tend not to be deciduous. The gymnosperms represent a step up the evolutionary ladder among trees. One mark of this is their ability, as a group, to adapt to many environmental conditions. They circle the globe from about sixty degrees north and south latitude to the tropics. Some—like the mangrove—grow under the wettest conditions, others—like the paloverde—grow under the driest. Changing climates and thoughtless destruction by humans have reduced the world's forests to a fraction of what they once were.

Trees come in just about all sizes and shapes. Some are tall, others squat. Conifers tend to be conical; hardwoods are shaped like fans, lollypops, or umbrellas. But what trees share is far more important than what divides them. They are the largest and most magnificent in the world of green plants. And, like all green plants, they are food factories, or more specifically, electro-chemical treatment plants. The difference between trees and the others is that they perform their functions on such a magnificent scale.

How much of its food does a tree take from the soil as it grows? Practically none. A sixteenth-century Belgian physician demonstrated this. Jean Baptista van Helmont planted a willow which weighed five pounds in a pot that contained exactly two hundred pounds of dry soil. The tree was watered regularly. That's all. Five years later, the tree weighed 169 pounds, and the soil it grew in was within two ounces of its original weight.

A tree imports raw materials, manufactures food, gets rid of waste, and exports finished goods. By and large, it is its own customer. Using energy from the sun, it converts carbon dioxide and water into carbohydrates and oxygen. The process is called photosynthesis, and the food produced nourishes the tree, all other green plants, and the overwhelming majority of the animals on earth, including us.

The secret ingredient in photosynthesis is a substance called chlorophyll. This absorbs sunlight, primarily in the violet, blue, and red wavelengths, and it reflects green. Thus, we have green plants. The beautiful colors of autumn—reds, yellows, browns—are the leaves' true colors, and are seen because the chlorophyll has faded as its source has been cut off.

As in any manufacturing process, photosynthesis produces waste. The one most important to animal life is oxygen.

Oxygen combines directly with most elements—a process called oxidation, which is a slow form of combustion. So oxygen is the agent which, in combination with nutrients, fuels the engine of animal life. We breathe it in, it oxidizes our food, and releases the energy we need. We exhale one of our own waste products—carbon dioxide, which compound is essential to the tree.

Photosynthesis takes place in the leaves.

The average leaf is less than one-quarter millimeter thick, and contains an electro-chemical processing plant, an air conditioning system complete with automatic valving, two plumbing systems, and structural elements to support the whole thing.

A broadleaf is formed of two parts—the blade and a stem. The blade is covered by upper and lower skins which are coated with a waxy material that provides airproofing and waterproofing. Directly beneath the upper skin there are rows of cylindrical cells called palisades. Each tall palisade cell is filled with upwards of one hundred wafer-like cells called chloroplasts, which are made up of chlorophyll molecules. A loose mass of spongy cells lies under the palisade cells.

The underside of a leaf is covered with tiny pores called stomata. There may be about twenty-five to fifty thousand of these per square centimeter or there may be none. Each of the stomata has two guard cells that function as valves, allowing atmosphere to enter the leaf and water vapor to escape. Stomata are so small that, although water vapor escapes, the larger drop of water in the atmosphere cannot enter. The release of water vapor is called transpiration and is essential to the tree's existence.

The needles of coniferous trees do the same work as do the broadleafs, but are much less specialized. The end result is the same.

A network of veins threads through the spongy cells of a broadleaf. The veins are microscopic and extremely bunched-up. This network joins and rejoins throughout the leaf, much as a river grows as its side streams join the flow. The veins in a leaf are two-tiered, constituting the upper extremity of the tree's two plumbing systems. They are covered by a tough covering which protects them and supports the leaf.

Light, water, carbon dioxide, and trace minerals are needed for a leaf to work. Light is the source of energy. Water, carbon dioxide, and the minerals provide the raw materials.

The light, sunlight primarily, passes through the leaf's upper skin, and strikes the chloroplast wafers in the palisade cells. As each becomes charged with solar energy, another moves up. In effect, the chloroplasts are batteries that store electrical energy. To assure the optimal exposure to light, the leaf's stem can distort to turn the blade to the proper angle.

Energy from the light breaks down water in the leaf into hydrogen and oxygen. The hydrogen atoms stay in the leaf for use in food production. The oxygen is passed out through the stomata into the atmosphere as waste— except to the animals that breathe it.

The carbon dioxide that animals breathe out, plus that from other sources, enters the leaf as part of the air passing through the stomata. There it bonds to the hydrogen atoms in the palisade cells, and with certain trace minerals, begins producing food for the tree.

The air that passes into the leaf contains water vapor that saturates the spongy cells lying below the palisade cells. This sponge serves as a reservoir, storing the water. As needed, it condenses on the palisade cells and dissolves the carbohydrates—sugars—oozing through the cell walls. The sugar is converted into starches, fats, oils and proteins.

A square yard of leaf—and a mature deciduous tree carries about two thousand square yards of leaves—can produce about one gram of carbohydrate per hour. The tree manufactures more than one and one-half tons of food in a growing season.

The leaf gets first call on the food it produces, much as an animal's heart receives the first of the oxygenated blood it has pumped. The tree's food then circulates to nourish new growth and serve the reproductive functions of the tree. Surplus food is stored for future use in the tree's roots, buds, and wood.

Water rising from the tree's roots and the sugary

solution leaving the leaves are known as sap. The water is crude sap, the sugar elaborated sap. They move through the tree in two separate plumbing systems. One transports water aloft to the leaves, the other takes food to the growing parts of the tree and to storage areas. The elaborated sap moves much more slowly than the upward-moving crude sap.

The elaborated and crude saps are carried in cells within a microscopically thin group of cells called the cambium. This film of living tissue lies between the wood and bark.

Elaborated sap travels in the *outer* layer of cambium cells, called the phloem, lying against the bark. It consists of cylindrically shaped cells that fit together, end-to-end. The sap filters through perforations in the ends of the cells and is drawn by osmosis throughout the tree.

Crude sap is transported up through cells lying on the *inner* side of the cambium. The live tissue in a tree is mainly water, which makes up roughly one-half of a newly cut log. Eighty percent of the weight of leaves and twigs in the growing season is water, all of which comes from the tree's roots.

As critical as water is to photosynthesis and the flow of dissolved trace minerals, only about one percent is used in photosynthesis. Some of the "excess" keeps the tree's living cells in the bloated condition needed for health. If these cells dry out, they harden and the tree starves.

Most of the tree's "surplus" water passes out through the leaves' stomata into the atmosphere, a process called transpiration.

Although the tree gets its water from the roots, it is not pumped up to the leaves. This is physically impossible. An efficient suction pump, such as the tree was assumed to be until relatively recently, can lift water only about thirty-four feet, at which point, the weight of the water and of the atmosphere balance. So a thirty-five-foot tree would be in trouble.

The secret to how water gets to leaves is transpiration.

Molecules of all stable materials want to stay attached to each other. In liquids and gases, this need is so great that if one molecule is displaced, another will move in to replace it, and another to replace that one, and so on. A tree draws its water up from the roots by molecular bonding. For this to work, one molecule of water must be lost in order for another to be attracted. The tree loses this molecule through transpiration. As the molecule of water vapor passes out through a stoma, another is drawn into the leaf from the plumbing system, and another moves in to replace that one. The chain reaction passes down the tree all the way to the smallest rootlet. The cumulative effect of all the stomata on all the leaves on just one tree is impressive. A mature maple tree can haul up two hundred gallons of water per hour, and one acre of trees can transpire more than eight thousand gallons of water into the atmosphere in one day.

But even the power of molecular bonding has its limits. Eventually its ability to lift water is balanced by the downward pull of gravity. The world's tallest trees, Australia's 375-foot mountain eucalyptus and California's redwoods, probably are pushing the limits.

The tree's system of roots is roughly the same shape as what is above ground. Just as branches divide into progressively smaller twigs, so the roots branch out until they are tiny rootlets. But the smallest twigs are large enough to support buds and leaves, and barring disease or accident, will live for the tree's lifetime. The smallest roots are single-celled "hairs" that live only a few hours.

The tree's roots serve two purposes. They anchor the tree and absorb water and dissolved minerals. The typical anchoring method is for the tree to drive one or more tap roots straight into the ground, with a network of other roots branching off. Some trees have root systems that lie just below the surface, and to compensate for the lack of tap roots, the tree develops a massive root network that spreads out laterally. The California sequoia anchors itself this way.

The bald cypress of the American southeast grows in swamps. It sends out roots that intermesh like a heavy anchor sunk in the soft ooze.

Some trees, like the banyan, send down roots from the trunk and branches. One banyan tree in India had a main trunk forty-two feet in circumference, plus 232 secondary roots, some of which were ten feet around.

The second function of roots is to absorb the water and dissolved minerals. The tip of each rootlet is capped by a hard cap that pushes through the soil, probing for moisture. Immediately behind the cap is the root's growth zone. Here the cells elongate and divide, and push the probing root cap through the soil.

When water is found, countless thousands of single-cell hair-like filaments suddenly grow immediately behind the root cap. They absorb the moisture, which, attracted by molecular bonding, passes back, molecule-by-molecule, into the tree's plumbing. These tiny hairs play out their role and die in just a few days. How many of these root hairs does a tree have? It's unlikely we will ever know. A nineteenth-century study of a single rye plant (grass) discovered 378 miles of roots, fourteen million separate roots, and fourteen *billion* root hairs.

The root tip is one of four places where the tree is alive. The three others are the buds, leaves, and the cambium.

A tree wears a "glove" that lies just beneath the bark and stretches from the topmost twig to the deepest rootlet. It is called the cambium, and is a thin layer of living tissue. It is the tissue through which water climbs up from the root and dissolved sugars seep down from the leaves.

The tree's bark grows on the outside of the cambium, and serves the tree as a skin, enclosing it from top to bottom. It insulates from heat and cold and prevents desiccation. It protects from insect invasion, and serves as a bandage over wounds.

As new layers of bark are formed during the tree's growth, the outer layers harden and thicken. These layers constitute what we know as cork. Its thickness varies among species. Birch trees have practically none, sequoias up to two feet. When I was in Spain, I got to see the famous cork oaks and watched workers harvest them.

The inner bark of the cork oak is an especially uniform tissue that regenerates itself after harvesting. After the outer, rough bark is stripped off, this inner layer forms up to one or two inches of the fine, commercial grade of cork each year.

The cork oak (*Quercus suber*) is a native of the Mediterranean region. Spain alone has more than two million acres of these trees. The cork is unique because of its tiny, air-filled cells, which make the cork watertight and an excellent insulator. When cork is cut, the surface is seen to be made up of closely packed half spheres, each of which acts like a suction cup. So cork, in addition to its insulating and waterproofing properties, is also skid-proof and wear-resistant. Cork weighs only one-fifth as much as water, and has been used since Roman times for buoyancy in everything from fish nets to life preservers.

Cork is harvested by stripping. The tree is girdled at a designated distance up the trunk, and great care is taken not to damage the cambium cells. Then a vertical cut is made with a special saw or knife, and the cork is carefully peeled from the trunk with the use of wedges. It is then boiled to remove the tannin. Properly managed and harvested, a tree will produce cork for twenty or more years.

The tree's wood is created from the cambium's inner layer cells. It is hard, dead, and constitutes about ninety-nine percent of the tree's bulk. It is made up of cellulose and lignin. Lignin fills the space between the bundles of cellulose molecules, creating what we know as wood.

Nutrients are stored in ducts called "rays," which radiate laterally in the wood. Eventually the ducts become clogged, which results in dark streaks that radiate out from the center.

As the tree grows upward—elongates—it adds girth at the same time. Elongation takes place at twig ends and the tips of roots. Girth is added by cell division in the cambium.

The tree grows taller and its branches longer at the ends of the trunk and twigs, where buds that formed during the previous season suddenly burst, stimulated by the springtime light and heat. Conifers have terminal buds on the ends of trunk and branches, which causes the trees' cone shape. On broad-leaved trees, the main branches are shoots off the trunk, which results in the fan or lollypop shape. A tree trunk does not push up nor its branches out as they elongate. A nail driven into a tree trunk five feet above the ground will be five feet off the ground for the tree's lifetime.

The tree adds girth through cell division in the cambium as they swell and divide, slide apart, then lie side-by-side. The daily increase in girth can be measured. During daylight hours, when transpiration is high, the diameter of the trunk can decrease. But during the night, when transpiration stops, water fills the tree's cells, and the trunk and branches increase in diameter.

Spring wood, formed early in the growing season, is soft, light-colored, and filled with the hollow cells that carry water up from the roots. When the season is warm and moist, wide bands of spring wood are produced. In cool, dry springs, the bands are narrower. During the summer, wood production slows and eventually stops. A narrow band of dense, dark wood is packed against the outer edge of the spring wood. Year after year, the tree increases its girth by adding alternate layers of spring and summer wood. They make up what is called sapwood. The inner layers of sapwood are gradually impregnated with resins, gums and tannin. They harden, die, and are transformed into the dense, hard center of the tree, the heartwood.

The sequence of light-colored spring wood and dark summer wood make up the annular (circular) rings. Generally, their total number is also the tree's age. But there are exceptions caused by drought, disease, insects, and the topography of the land.

The tree's growth is regulated by an enzyme called auxin which is made in buds and leaves near the terminal ends of twigs. When the first buds open in spring, auxin begins to travel toward the roots in the phloem. It saturates the entire tree, tiptop to outermost rootlet, setting off the season's growth.

Auxin is light-sensitive, so it moves toward the shaded parts of the tree during the daylight hours. Thus, it stimulates growth on the dark sides of leaf stems. This, in turn, causes the leaf to twist toward the light, exposing the largest leaf surface to the source of solar energy. Auxin is also partly responsible for trees shedding their leaves. In autumn, as the light level and temperature decrease, the flow of auxin slows, reducing the tree's functioning. With its supply of water and dissolved minerals stopped, the leaf dies. A layer of cells at the base of the stem dissolves, and the leaf falls.

In addition to growing and staying healthy, a tree must reproduce itself.

The tree's seeds are conceived in the flower buds. The female component in seed production is the egg, the male component, pollen, which contains the sperm. The flower buds of most forest species are dormant in winter, then bloom the following spring.

The flowers of deciduous trees usually appear in spring before leafing, but there are exceptions. Pollination occurs shortly after the flowers reach maturity, but then there can be a delay before fertilization that can range from one or two days to more than a year.

The smallest seed—which is microscopic—in the plant world is that of the rhododendron. The largest is the coconut, which can weigh several pounds. The fruit we eat—apples, pears, peaches, and so forth—are actually the trees' ovaries surrounding fertilized seeds. Sometimes there is one seed per ovary, as in a peach, sometimes many, as in apples.

The seeds leave their parent trees in many ways. Some have one or more wings and fly. Some have parachutes and float to earth. Some are encased in burrs that get caught in animals' fur. Some are inside tough cases that pass through the digestive tracts of animals and fall to earth in their droppings. Some seeds float on the water, some are on stilts that become embedded in the mud.

There are seeds that are "shot" from the parent tree, and there are seeds that attract rodents that harvest them and bury them in the earth.

The odds against a seed's landing in the right place at the right time are astronomical, so trees produce seeds in equally astronomical numbers. A ponderosa pine can produce sixty thousand in one season, a Douglas fir, 180,000. A mature alder, in its productive life—usually about thirty years—can produce three million seeds.

Trees have been on earth in one form or another for 350 million years. They have seen countless species of plants and animals fall into extinction. From humble beginnings in Devonian swamps, trees have reached out to conquer the world and become its most impressive form of plant life.

Chapter 6

About the time I left Lambert Gardens, I began planting nursery stock on a piece of idle land my wife's family owned east of Portland, thinking that sometime I might go into business for myself. I didn't have money so I just planted anything. I remember planting several hundred suckers of common lavender lilacs. Of course they grew well. I moved them, spaced them a little bit and just let them grow. In three or four years, they were big enough to sell. I put ads in the newspaper for old-fashioned lilacs, and sold all of them for three dollars and fifty cents each. That was quite a bit of money in those days. I also planted cuttings of weeping willows. They grew well and later I charged twenty dollars for a large willow delivered and planted.

Over the years, I continued planting whatever I could get my hands on. Sometimes I didn't hit it right, but somehow managed to get rid of all that nursery stock. Maybe a nurseryman would want a lot of the plants and I'd make him a price and clean out the whole area. The land out there was among the best in the state for nursery stock. In fact, Gresham, Oregon, is sitting on some of the best topsoil in the country. For many years, it was the nursery area of Oregon. Now the town is developing rapidly, covering this soil with asphalt and concrete.

Some day, hopefully not too far in the future, we as a nation will come to grips with the destruction of our fertile land. It always distresses me to see housing tracts and shopping malls covering what was good farmland. At some point, responsible ecological considerations have to get as much consideration as purely economic ones.

For example, it makes no ecological sense to build tracts of houses on good, fertile farmland simply because it is cheaper to build there than on hills, which are at best marginal for farming.

Of course, there has to be equal consideration given to proper hillside building. One of the worst examples of hillside building can be found in Los Angeles. There, entire hillsides and canyons are scalped and terraced like layer cakes, and houses are built on each terrace, one per terrace if the neighborhood is an affluent one. This practice, aside from being unspeakably ugly, is like building a time bomb. There has been a great drought in southern California for several years, which has lulled developers into the false idea that they can put houses anyplace. But climate is a constantly changing phenomenon, and one of these years the drought will end. Then the area will revert to its normal weather pattern of dry, hot summers and wet winters. In fact, as I write this, the state is emerging from one of its wettest winters. This could lead to disaster.

For tens of thousands of years, the Mediterranean climate that southern California enjoys has allowed ground cover to adapt to the climate and soil. But it is primarily chaparral—a dwarf forest, for one of the characteristics of a chaparral is its stunted size. The tallest plants seldom exceed twenty feet, and most are much shorter. Another characteristic feature of a chaparral is the leaves that grow on the plants. Most are small, tough and leathery, features that reduce water loss through transpiration and evaporation. In a typical southern California chaparral community, there are about two dozen species of plants, each of which contributes to the entire community.

The chaparral grows most vigorously in winter—November through April—in southern California's wet season. In late spring, the plants slip back into the semi-dormancy that will protect them during the hot, dry season to follow.

The plants of the chaparral often suffer from wildfires in the seasonal late summer drought. After several years of no fires, the hillsides are thick with plants that are rosin-rich and tinder dry. The chaparral has adapted to this. Not only does it suffer wildfires kindly, it requires them to cleanse itself.

The secret of the chaparral's regeneration after fire lies in the roots. While upper stems and branches of the plants are destroyed by fire, the roots live on. In just a few springtimes after a fire, new shoots have pushed up among the whitened skeletons of manzanita, scrub oak, squawbush, poison oak, ceanothus, toyon, holly-leaved cherry, mountain mahogany, laurel, sumac, black sage, chemise, and greasewood. The chaparral is once again the dominant plant community of the southern California hillsides.

The chaparral's network of roots also performs another function. Chaparral country gets only about ten inches or so of precipitation per normal year. That's good news for the tens of thousands of sun worshippers who live on southern California's hillsides and canyon floors. The bad news is that those ten inches come in the space of just a few weeks. When they fall on hillsides still covered by the chaparral, the resulting runoff is slowed, allowed to percolate into the soil and to seep slowly down to the canyons where it runs in to riverbeds, with little disturbance of existing vegetation. But let those hillsides be stripped of their cover and bulldozed into the terraces so beloved by developers, and it's a different story. With nothing to stop the runoff but houses and lawns, the water tears the terraces apart and carries them into the canyons, where the flood rips out whatever growth there is, along with the pretty little houses. This happens again and again in southern California, and still developers 'doze the hills and fill the canyons with houses.

Of course, southern California is merely an extreme example of what is happening all over our country as good, rich farmland is covered with asphalt, and hillsides are sculpted by bulldozers. There has to be a better ethic in building, one that respects the integrity of land that has taken tens of thousands of years to achieve whatever understanding it has with the forces of nature.

After I left Lambert Gardens in 1939, I was ready to get into the nursery and landscaping business full bore. I had served a long apprenticeship in the technical aspects of cultivating plants and in the sales end of the business with Mr. Lambert, so I figured I might as well give it a try.

I never did have a large business; no more than ten or twelve employees at a time. Neither did I focus on straight retail sales, but tried to get landscaping contracts. I'd take prospective customers out to see other landscaping jobs I had done, and let the quality of the work speak for itself.

We did highway work for the State Highway Department, local and regional parks, shopping centers and other commercial developments, urban renewal projects around town, and street tree plantings. My office was in my home, and I used a storage area in Portland where I had bought a couple of lots. I had a landscaping business from 1939 until I retired in 1977.

The nursery/landscape business provided funds to raise my family and set aside a bit for my retirement. It also increased my knowledge about trees and multiplied my passion to save them many times over. Now and then it also provided a laugh, and even some embarrassments.

I met Bill Gruber a little before World War II. He had immigrated from Germany shortly after the First World War, and was a friend of my first wife. Bill was a fantastic person—an inventer, a naturalist, forest ranger, business associate, and a good friend. During his years with the Forest Service in Oregon, he came to love the great forests that grew in the Coast Range and the Cascades. He became involved in the development of many of the scenic trails we have in the Columbia River Gorge. (I have hiked just about all of them, often in Bill's company.) During the Second World War, he was interned, although there was never any indication that he was anything but loyal to the United States. He was released in 1945 and returned to Oregon.

Bill invented a method of taking and showing stereo photos, which he named Viewmaster. It became a worldwide success. Now and then I would go along when

Bill went out to take pictures for his Viewmaster reels. Once we went by boat as far up the Snake River as was possible in those days. That trip through Hell's Canyon was one of the high points of my outdoor life. There was another that could easily qualify as a low point.

We were going up on Mt. Rainier—one of the few Cascade peaks I hadn't climbed—so Bill could photograph windflowers (anemones). Not that we would be going to the top. Bill wanted to visit some of the lovely little alpine meadows that occur up on the slopes. That's where many of the wildflowers grow in the moist, fertile soil. On the way we stopped at a store and bought some groceries. When we reached our campsite, Bill went out mushroom hunting. Among his many talents, Bill was a mycologist, and his photos of mushrooms were much in demand by scientists. He came back with a small pail or a hat full, and said, "Frank, tomorrow morning I'm going to make you a delicious breakfast of sausage and mushrooms." I climbed into my sleeping bag thinking about that great breakfast my friend was going to prepare, and I woke to the wonderful aroma of food cooking. Bill Gruber was making good on his promise. He said that the variety of mushrooms we were eating was the best kind of vegetative steak available. Beef was one thing; these mushrooms were something else. They sure were.

About mid-afternoon I began to feel queasy. That evening, Bill opened a large can of beef stew. I ate and immediately headed for the bushes to vomit. It went on and on until I was throwing up blood. So was Bill.

"Frank, we're getting out of here right now!" Bill said.

On the way home, we stopped at a hospital where somebody gave me some pills. The next thing I remember was being stopped by the state police. Then I passed out and didn't come to until several days later, in my own bed at home. Bill Gruber was as sick as I was. I never did learn what kind of mushroom he had fed us.

That disaster wasn't the end of my involvement with Bill Gruber. A few years later, he insisted that we grow mushrooms. He claimed that we would get rich in just one season. They were selling for a dollar a pound, an unbelievable price in those days. I had access to a vacant concrete house that Gruber said was ideal for growing mushrooms. My first job, said Gruber, was to gather the medium in which to grow the mushrooms. I was to visit riding academies and wherever else the very best horses were raised and housed. They had to be the *very* best in order to get the finest material in which to plant the mushroom spawn we would buy. I guess I visited just about every riding academy and fancy horse ranch in the Portland area. I was after fresh, used bedding straw that was soaked with urine and manure. I cleaned stalls and dug into manure piles all over town. Then I trucked the stuff back to the concrete house and spread it outside to "cure." I was creating an enormous compost heap. I piled it, raked it, turned it so it got air and didn't heat up so much that its "livability," as Bill Gruber called it, was destroyed. I spent the entire summer collecting mushroom spawn "medium." When the pile was large enough to meet Gruber's standards, I built racks in the concrete house. We loaded them with compost and spread fine sand on top of it. When the growing beds met Gruber's standards, he sent away for the mushroom spawn. He strictly dictated the humidity and temperature I was to maintain. I was beginning to dream about the money.

We didn't get one mushroom, not even one button!

Although the mushroom crop was a failure, Bill Gruber was enthusiastic and persuasive about the importance of tree planting. His enthusiasm and knowledge went far to move me in the direction my life would take. Despite the fact that he had almost killed me, and then made me spend a whole summer shoveling horse manure, I have always valued his opinions.

Early in my landscaping business, I got a call from a lady who wanted a tree removed from her yard. I went out with a crew to get them started on felling this big poplar, then cleaning up the debris. I left to get on with another project. When I came back to help the crew clean up, the lady came out of the house screaming. The men had cut down the wrong tree! This really was shocking and made me feel really bad. As for the client, she didn't pay for cutting the wrong tree, but didn't charge me for doing it, so the project came out a wash except for the crew's wages.

I worked at the shipyard throughout the war on the swing shift. This left me a little time to conduct the nursery business, and I managed to keep it going.

In late 1944 or '45 I collected some cuttings from an English holly tree growing on my in-laws' property. I made a wreath and some sprays and took them as gifts to an old friend who was in the wreath-making business. He figured I was trying to sell it to him, and said something about coals to Newcastle, but I assured him it was just a gift. "You've been a good friend and I wanted to give you something," I said.

The following spring he called me and said, "Frank, I wasn't very nice to you about the holly. I looked through it and some was nice. I'm going to need several tons next fall. Do you want to supply at least some of it?" And that's how I expanded my nursery business to include cutting holly.

In addition to my friend, I also got a contract from a major holly-shipping company in Portland, so from about mid-October until shortly before Christmas each year, I was very busy.

When I get involved with something, I like to learn all I can about it. So I read books on holly, and learned there are about three hundred species spread around the world from Central and South America, to Africa, Europe and Australia. Fifteen of the species are native to North America, but the popular English and variegated varieties used in Christmas wreathes and decorations are imports.

The use of holly for decorative purposes goes back to well before Christianity. In Rome, the practice was part of the festival of Saturnalia, which honored the god Saturn in mid-December. In northern Europe, evergreens, including holly, were hung indoors in Teutonic households as a refuge for wood spirits from the cold.

To assure a supply of holly, I decided to travel north along the Pacific coast from the Oregon/California border, to Seattle. I'd begin in the spring, looking for good holly trees of either the English or variegated varieties. When I spotted a likely prospect, I'd offer to buy the crop from the owner, and actually make a substantial deposit. This was a bit risky because I didn't know what might happen between then and the fall. There could be a crop failure; birds might eat all the berries; or other problems might occur. But I wanted the people to feel committed and to understand that I was serious.

To spread out the cutting a bit, I arranged for cold storage of the cuttings from mid-October. We cut holly for more than twenty-five years, and in that time I probably touched just about every place in western Oregon and Washington. I mention this because all that travel up and down the Northwest showed me a disaster firsthand. It didn't happen suddenly, and there was no great public outcry at the time, but what I saw happening made our corner of the nation, the country, and the entire world a little bit poorer.

The strip of land we call the Pacific Northwest, stretching about a thousand miles from northern California to the northern tip of British Columbia and inland to the crest of the Cascades, contains the most diverse forest in the world. There were, at one time, tens of millions of acres of fir, cedar, hemlock, redwood, sequoia, and spruce. Until the turn of the twentieth century, they were largely virgin forests. Initially the native residents had neither the tools nor the desire to cut them, at least in large numbers. North-coast Indians did build their homes and boats of wood from the trees, mainly the huge western cedars that grew along the moist, warm coastlands. But these activities made no dent in the vast forests covering the land.

Now and then white navigators and explorers dropped anchor in the bays that dotted the coast, and sometimes they felled trees to repair their ships. But for the most part the forests went undisturbed, existing in the slow cycle of birth, growth, and death that had existed since the last of the glacier retreated about ten thousand years ago.

With the appearance of settlers from the East in the mid-nineteenth century, the situation began to change. These settlers were farmers for the most part, and needed cleared land on which to grow their crops. So the forests, at least those on the land the settlers wanted, were felled, and much of their beautiful, straight-grained wood was tossed onto the burn pile. But still the impact on the forests overall was minor. There were so many trees, there was no possibility of cutting all of them. They would go on forever.

'Forever' lasted just a few years. The first big assault on the forests of the Northwest came with the insatiable appetite for lumber of the thousands of people swarming into California in response to the discovery of gold. After cutting most of the useable trees on the west slopes of the Sierra Nevada, the people looked north to the great untouched forests. Soon, millions of board feet of lumber were headed south. And still, because of the enormous number of trees in that stretch of land, the effect on the forests was minimal—noticeable yes—but minimal.

Then, around the beginning of the twentieth century, the nation's other great forests, those around the Great Lakes, were gone, all cut, just as, in an earlier time, the forests of New England had disappeared because of overcutting. The lumber barons had promised that the Great Lakes' forests would last one thousand years. In fact, they said, there were so many of them they would never disappear.

'Never' took about seventy-five years.

When the last of the commercially valuable trees were cut in the former forests of the Great Lakes, the timber barons and the people who worked for them headed west. The big bosses knew about the forests waiting there to make them even richer. But the lumberjacks (who would be called loggers in their new home) had never seen such trees—trees fifteen feet in diameter and more than two hundred feet tall. Forests so thick with trees, ferns, and fallen logs, that a person couldn't walk through. Trees that crowded each other from the ocean's edge inland for up to 150 miles. Before they had actually come west, the lumberjacks figured these were more stories like the Paul Bunyan legends, products of active imaginations and maybe too many shots of whiskey.

But when they finally saw the trees they became instant believers, and set to work. Years later when I was driving around looking for holly trees, the results of that early logging were still plain. There were huge areas where the native trees still hadn't regenerated. In those early days of logging in the Northwest there were no legal demands that an area be replanted after logging, and no requirements about cleaning up. So these enormous stretches of land were cluttered with the rotting trees that had been too small or crooked or whatever for the loggers. The erosion was bad and what growth there was consisted mainly of brush. Here and there a lonely old fir or hemlock stuck up out of the undergrowth. There were old railroad beds that had been abandoned when all the trees were cut. The companies had ripped up the tracks and taken them elsewhere, I suppose, probably to the next logging site. Because as one block of land was destroyed, operations were moved farther up the mountains. They were still going on of course, but by the time I was doing my holly cruising, most logging operations were far out of public sight. Everything else had been cut long ago.

In the later years of the holly project, in addition to signing up individuals who had holly trees, I began buying from the small farms. When holly became a major Christmas crop and people discovered that it grew very well in the Northwest, small farmers planted orchards of the crop. Nurserymen who had young holly trees to sell promoted the plantings for obvious reasons. They assured the farmers that in this case money *could* grow on trees— holly trees. "Plant an acre of holly and guarantee your children a college education," they would advertise. What they didn't mention was that holly is a slow-growing tree, that takes about fifteen years to come to the point where harvesting can begin. So by that time, the owner was usually approaching old age; maybe his health was failing, or he hadn't taken care of the trees properly, or he didn't know how to market the crop. There weren't very many small growers who sent their children to college on the profits they made from holly. There are no easy dollars to be made in agriculture, so if I offered to care for the trees during the growing season, and take the entire crop, the owners usually were overjoyed.

I was surprised to find so many holly trees growing along the Oregon coast from Seaside to Canon Beach and Cape Lookout. But strangest of all was the number of holly trees I saw in the mountains and deep in the forest. At the most unexpected times and places, there would be a holly tree with its rich green leaves and red berries. I finally figured out how they came to be in these places. Birds. Robins, especially, are fond of holly berries. The seeds stay undigested and pass out in the birds' droppings. Much of a natural forest's regeneration takes place this way.

Another good source of holly was cemeteries. The best were those that had been around for a long time. Often they had holly trees that had been part of the original landscaping, and caretakers were happy to have somebody trim them. But in one case, we didn't have such a pleasant reception.

I located an especially nice, very large holly tree in a cemetery in Eugene, a town more than two hours drive from home. I found the owner, an attorney whose family owned the plot on which the tree was growing. I identified myself as a holly buyer and an expert at trimming the tree, and the owner prepared a document that allowed me to trim his tree and keep the foliage. But when I returned to the cemetery, the custodian drove me off, arguing that he didn't want anybody trimming trees in *his* cemetery. The following Saturday, my crew and I went back early in the morning and set to work. The tree was perhaps forty feet tall. We cut it back to a reasonable height, and shaped it. As we were finishing, the custodian came by, stopped his car and began to argue, threatening to call the police. I explained that we had permission from the tree's owner, and were going to finish our work. The custodian demanded to see the permission. I refused, thinking that he might destroy it, and anyway, I had forgotten to bring it with me. He grumbled a bit, but left shouting that he didn't want to see us on this property ever again. I figured it would take several years for that tree to produce another good crop, so his threat didn't mean very much, and we got more than five hundred pounds of beautiful holly from that one tree.

Sometimes, owners were not as cooperative as the attorney had been. I knew of one excellent tree and went to see the owner. "No sir!" he snapped when I asked to buy the holly crop. The next year I went back and got the same answer. "No sir!" And the next. And the next. Then came the year when I knocked on the door and a lady answered. She smiled and said, "Young man, your persistence has paid off. My husband died this year and I will let you have the holly." The sad part of the story is that when we went to harvest the tree, insects or disease had beaten us to it. The holly was worthless.

Once in a while I would run into especially good luck when I was out scouting for holly. One time I ran into a beautiful tree growing on a lot with an abandoned house and a magnificent view of Mt. Hood. I tracked down the owner and called him. Not only was he willing to sell the holly, he also offered me the house. After some negotiation we settled on a price, and I had a piece of property that, over the years, appreciated in value.

One time, in traveling the state looking for holly, I found a tree near Tillamook that was the largest variegated holly I had ever seen. It must have been fifty to sixty feet tall, with a trunk that, at chest height, had a diameter of two feet. I thought that such a specimen deserved recognition, so I asked a forester friend, Ernie Kolbe, to help. We appealed to the national office that establishes records, and soon had the Tillamook specimen registered as the largest holly tree in the United States. I don't know if it is still standing.

In some cases I would take care of holly trees all summer and fall that I had contracted to harvest that spring. In some instances, I helped to propagate especially good trees. Thanks to my years in the propagation house at Lambert Gardens, I knew quite a bit about how to have a tree reproduce itself.

Holly trees, like many species, will reproduce from cuttings and through layering. The cutting method, of course, involves planting small pieces of twigs, which will take root and grow if the process is done properly. Layering involves bending a branch into the ground, covering it with soil and holding it in place with bent lengths of wire or pipe. The area is kept watered and eventually that portion of the branch will send down roots. The section can then be cut from the main tree and planted on its own. Many variegated holly trees, which are one of the most highly prized for wreaths and sprays, are started this way.

I had contacts with Mr. Lambert, my former boss, during my nursery and landscaping business days. He might call me if he had a job so large he couldn't handle it by himself. But we remained competitors, and I must say a person had to stay on his toes when he was competing with Andrew B. Lambert.

One time after the war, I bid on an Urban Renewal landscaping contract that required the planting of large, eastern oak trees. There weren't many of these around. I knew that Lambert had some growing in his nursery, so I went up to talk with him about them. After I explained my needs, he said he'd sell them to me for seventy-five dollars each. I entered my bid based on this figure. After winning the contract, I went back to Mr. Lambert to buy the trees. "Oh Frank, I made a mistake," he said. "Those trees are 150 dollars each." That put the fat in the fire. The architect for the project and I traveled the entire region looking for eastern oaks that pleased him. None did. Then I learned that Mr. Lambert had sold the property on which the original trees were growing. I went to the new owner and asked to buy them. "Oh sure. I'll let them go for twenty-five dollars a piece." After I moved them, Mr. Lambert found out about the deal and was very angry with me.

But his anger didn't last, or if it did, he was pragmatic enough to swallow it when he needed my help. A little later, he won a landscaping contract. But the architect on the job had it in for him, and Mr. Lambert thought that he wouldn't get any of his work approved. So he pleaded with me to help. I went down to the job, did the required planting, and the architect approved it.

That's the way it was between Mr. Lambert and me.

Chapter 7

I suppose that from the time I was a teenager, I was moving in the direction of ReTree. That is, I was devoting more and more of my time to planting trees, sometimes by myself and sometimes with a group of my Scouts, and at times as part of other groups.

In 1929 or '30, I joined the Demolay, a group of young men sponsored by the Masons. One of their annual statewide conclaves was scheduled to be held in Bend, a small timber town on the eastern slope of the Cascades. Today it is one of the fastest growing cities, not only in Oregon, but in the entire West, and logging has given way to tourism and skiing as the main industries. In the early 1930s, however, the highway to Bend was a narrow, twisting, two-lane road that snaked its way across the mountains. Most people traveled to Bend by train, which is what the Portland contingent of the Demolay did.

One of the adult leaders who went along was a tall, handsome forester named Albert Wizendanger. He worked for the Forest Service in the Mt. Hood National Forest, and had quite a reputation for influencing college students to consider forestry as a career. He also visited elementary and high schools speaking to students about the important roles forests played in their lives, and what constituted proper behavior in these forests.

On the way to Bend, Mr. Wizendanger talked with the boys about his favorite subject, the planting of trees. Of course, he was trying to recruit them, and, as I say, he was very convincing. At the conclave, he suggested that the organization sponsor tree plantings on a statewide basis. He was so persuasive that the assembly voted to

assess each member of the Demolay in Oregon an
additional thirty-five cents a year to help fund the project.
Instead of annual dues of three dollars, they would pay
three dollars and thirty-five cents. It seems a ridiculously
small amount these days, but you must remember that
back then, when a skilled tradesman's wages were about
one dollar a day, and kids like us earned far, far less, that
thirty-five cents represented a hefty sum.

Mr. Wizendanger suggested a planting site on the slopes
of Mt. Hood for the first tree planting. Many of those
Douglas firs that we Demolay boys and Albert
Wisendanger planted are gone. When the new highway
was built, they were bulldozed out of the way. About five
years ago, I took Mr. Wizendanger, who was then in his
nineties, and my granddaughter, Victoria Lockyear, to
look for our trees. A forester from the Zig Zag ranger
station went along with us and he took along an increment
borer. We wanted to determine if any of the trees we
found were the right age to be those we had planted
almost sixty years earlier.

We found several trees in the area of the project, and
the count of annular rings taken by the borer indicated
that they could be our trees. But who knows? The sign
that had marked the site was gone, and the highway had
taken out so many of the trees, it was almost impossible
to say whether these were the trees we had planted in our
youth. I even visited the Demolay state headquarters to
learn if there were any records of that little forest. There
were no records and nobody knew anything about them
or the forest.

But I'd like to think that, up there in the thick Douglas
fir forests, there are at least a few of the trees we planted
when we were young.

When you plant a tree, you make a statement about
the future. That is one of the magnificent things about
trees. Because they far outlive one human lifespan, they
seem to last forever. A friend of mine recently had to cut
up a great Douglas fir that had blown over during a bad
wind-storm. After chain sawing through the butt, he

counted the annular rings. There were 130 of them. That fir tree had been growing long before there were space rockets, radios, motion pictures, airplanes, or automobiles. It had been a two-year-old seedling when Abraham Lincoln was assassinated. At the turn of this century it was a tall, mature tree, producing seeds of its own to keep the forest replenished. How it escaped the unrestricted logging that swept through that part of the state like a plague of locusts will never be known. And who knows how it managed to endure wildfires and storms and droughts during all those years? It lived a long time from our human perspective, yet when it finally went down in its 130th year, that tree was still just a kid. A Douglas fir can live up to one thousand years under the right conditions.

Impressive as that is, it still is a mere eyewink of time compared with the age of the oldest trees on earth. These are the bristlecone pines, a species of gnarled conifers growing between 9,500 and 11,500 feet above sea level in the shallow, rocky, alkaline soil of a few desert mountains in the American Southwest. The growing season at the high point of the tree's range is short, about forty-five days from late June until mid-August. The trees add perhaps one inch of girth per century, and in particularly unfavorable years, do not grow at all.

Bristlecone pines have been on these mountains since the end of the last Ice Age. They are survivors of a time when saber-toothed cats, mammoths, dire wolves and giant ground sloths roamed the California grasslands, and a carnivorous bird called teratorn soared overhead on wings that spanned twelve feet.

As the climate dried and warmed, the trees in the valleys died off. Those that lived on the mountaintops mutated into forms adapted to the new, harsh conditions, with soil that is coarse and alkaline. There is little precipitation in these mountains because the Sierra Nevada block the moisture sweeping in from the ocean. A year of ten inches of rain is considered a wet one in these parts. Not only that, but the trees are exposed to winds that blast them with sand and ice particles, abrading away the bark and leaving just a narrow thread of living tissue snaking up the lee side of the trunk and branches.

In the White Mountains of California and other peaks in the Southwest, the bristlecones evolved into *Pinus longaeva*, and in the Rocky Mountains, into *P. aristata*. As a group, those growing in the upper extremes of their range bear little resemblance to the giant fir and cedar of my Pacific Northwest, nor to the magnificent hardwood species of eastern North America.

There are individual bristlecones still growing and producing viable seeds after four thousand years on Earth. One specimen on White Mountain is forty-six hundred years old. Another, on Wheeler Peak, Nevada, was well over five thousand years old when it was cut. That happened when a young man with the blood still dripping from his PhD diploma, tried to take a core from the tree and got his Swedish increment borer stuck. He prevailed on a Forest Service employee to fell the tree to free the instrument. That incident motivated Congress to place bristlecone pines under federal protection.

Walking among bristlecones can be a humbling experience. These very trees were growing here when humanity's first cities arose in Mesopotamia. They were seedlings when the Great Pyramids were built in Egypt. When Moses led his flock out of captivity, many of the trees in whose shade you rest were two thousand years old. And when the monks of Simonos Petra were building their monastery atop a great rock rising from the Aegean Sea, some of the bristlecones in the desert mountains of what would one day become the United States were already four thousand years old.

I suppose some people might say that planting trees is a way of trying to reach for immortality. I won't argue that. I admit it is comforting to think that down through the years, a child might lay his or her hand on a tree trunk and say, "My great grandfather planted this." Or, "My great, great grandfather planted this tree with a man who came to his school and told the children how important trees are to the Earth."

Scoutmaster Fred York, of Troop 104, was the ultimate outdoorsman. He had worked as a seasonal forester for the United States Forest Service, and knew Oregon's mountains and forests like the back of his hand. I suppose Fred was the single most important person to influence my early direction regarding tree planting. His enthusiasm for the forest resulted in a special group made up of local Scouts. In about 1934, eight or so of us older boys decided to establish a forestry club. The father of one of the boys helped me organize the group, and in his honor we named it after him—the Stuart Rice Foresters. Our goal was to learn trail building, forest mapping, fire control, and tree planting.

The Stuart Rice Foresters of Scouts from Troop 104 existed for three or four years. In that time, we learned a great deal about almost every aspect of forestry. I suppose that experience was instrumental in setting me on the course I have followed for more than sixty years, the attempt to plant trees on idle lands wherever in the world they might be.

The U.S. Forest Service was an important partner in those Boy Scout projects. They had the seedlings at the plant sites when we planted in the National Forest, and contributed them from their nursery at Wind River for projects outside the forest. Most of these were at the Boy Scouts' Camp Millard. The Scouts of Troop 104 made up the majority of the participants, but sometimes I was able to get several other troops involved also. By this time I was serving the Council as an assistant to the commissioner of the Sunrise District, so I had access to all the troops in that district. A District Commissioner in Scouting is a volunteer who coordinates administrative affairs of the troops in a designated area in the Council.

In Troop 104 we made tree planting projects part of the program. A project might take place as a part of an overnight hike, or just a one-day affair. Someone—a parent or adult volunteer—would provide transportation. The boys would bring their tools, and we would drive off to a spot in the mountains to plant trees. I suppose we planted several thousand during the years that the Stuart Rice Foresters existed.

Respect for nature has always been part of the Scout creed, but many of the boys who came out from town the first few times didn't know how this applied to their behavior in the woods. Almost every tree in the camp had been chopped into with hatchets and hacked with knives. In those days, one of the big things in Scouting was to learn how to use these tools, but nobody thought to teach the proper way to behave with them. I suppose nobody considered that a tree is a living thing with a spirit, a soul. Many of the boys thought it was just there to chop on.

I remember one little boy who came to camp for the first time. He found a nice little cedar, about eight feet tall, and cut every limb off that little tree, leaving just a few stubs. Then he spread the boughs on the ground for his bed. That was too much even for those of us who thought little of whacking off one or two branches. We lit into him and when he came back to camp in future years, he piled leaves and whatever else he could find (other than tree limbs!) to make himself a soft place to bed down.

I recall the incident because it was one of those turning points for several of us. We began to realize that the trees at Camp Millard were part of the experience we were out there to enjoy, and that they deserved the same respect we were to give wildlife. Thus I came to see in trees a nobility and grandeur that few other living things have for me.

Scoutmaster Fred York had a forester friend named R. Thomas Carter, who had been a regional forester in the Mt. Hood National Forest until an automobile accident left him paralyzed. He offered to teach the Stuart Rice Foresters, so we gathered twice a month at his home and, from his wheelchair, he shared what he had gleaned from his experience in the forests.

In 1950, after serving as Scoutmaster of Troop 104 for

twenty-seven years, Fred York resigned. I took over and guided the troop for the following nineteen years. Even after leaving that post, I stayed active in Scouting, and still am.

My friend, Bill Gruber, with whom I went on many camping trips, and in later years, shared the mushroom business venture, was instrumental in helping me organize a group of my Scouts into a tree planting unit. He suggested that, as part of our "Good Turn" activities, we plant trees in the newly formed Portland City Forest. Fred Clater, a forester with the U.S. Forest Service, the Izaak Walton League, and Bill Gruber were instrumental in getting the four-thousand-acre tract and convincing the city to set it aside as a forest. It lies in the heart of the city and is the largest such forest in a major city in the country—and our Scouts planted many of the trees.

The Scout tree plantings continued after I left Lambert Gardens and established my own nursery and landscaping business. Because of the contacts I established with nurseries and government agencies, I was able to get contributions of trees and seeds. Because I was so active in tree planting, I was tapped to serve on committees that organized the annual tree-planting activities of the various troops.

Ernie Kolbe, a forester, and the first director of the Portland-based World Forestry Center, encouraged me to expand my tree planting with children and to distribute seeds for scientific plantings around the world.

As these various projects increased, and I began devoting more and more of my time to tree planting, it became apparent that I needed an organization to give the work some structure. I also felt it would be better if I could announce that an organization was sponsoring each project rather than just Frank Lockyear.

When I retired from the landscaping business in the 1970s, my wife and I traveled quite a bit, and I usually tried to take seedlings or seeds to present to foresters or other government officials overseas. In 1973, we took a trip to Spain and Greece. I took along some seedlings to present to officials in the palace of Prince Carlos and in the city of Malaga. On the way over, the realization came to me that it was time to get about the business of organizing the tree-planting projects.

When I returned home, I contacted several people whose opinions I respected. I spoke with Glenn Jackson, a prominent Oregon citizen who was an orchardist, politician, and community activist; Guy Miller, at one time the local Scout executive; Don Richards and Mary Burns, attorneys; biologist Marjorie Meek; Robert Chapman, construction consultant and an old friend and former Scout in my troop; Dr. Sam Foster, a geneticist; Dr. Jim Lin, a forestry biometrician; and Rodger Starr, an accountant. Some of these people eventually joined our organization as members of its board. Through Sam Foster, I contacted the Oregon Society of Foresters and asked for their support. They were most enthusiastic, and have remained ReTree boosters. Over the years they have contributed the pins, ribbons, and certificates we give to children who join us in planting trees. ReTree has been fortunate also to have the support of several people important in forestry, the environment, and related fields. Dr. John Gordon, Dean of Yales's School of Forestry and Environmental Studies, was one of our early supporters. Nobel Laureate Dr. Norman Borlaug gave early support to our cause, and after our organization was functioning, wrote a most complimentary letter to me.

I asked these people about the feasibility of a nonprofit organization dedicated to planting trees. They thought it was a good idea. We named the new organization ReTree International—"ReTree" because that's what we wanted to do, "International" because of where we wanted to do it.

ReTree has three objectives:

The first is to plant forest trees on idle lands around the world wherever they will grow. These lands may be privately or publicly owned. Our only criteria are that they be capable of supporting trees, be set aside for the trees, and, hopefully, be protected from browsing and grazing animals such as cattle, pigs, goats, sheep, and wildlife.

It is obvious that the planting site must be able to support tree growth, so exceedingly rocky or dry sites are out. At the other extreme, soft marshlands, while great for certain sedges and grass, are hardly the place to try to grow trees. There must be adequate water for the seedlings, either through precipitation or irrigation. And if there is thick grass, it must be removed and kept from around each tree for the first growing season at least.

The site must be set aside for the trees. If the seedlings are to have any chance of survival, they must be free from human intrusion during the years that they are achieving maturity. But it is difficult to convince people in poverty-stricken countries to leave these lands alone, rather than to farm them or allow grazing livestock on them, or to cut them. I have seen hillsides in some third-world countries where all the growth has been cut for firewood. How can I blame the poor people who plunder the forests for fuel that eat the foliage? But the exploitive gathering of firewood and the concept of a growing, healthy forest are incompatible.

Finally, the matter of animals is especially critical in choosing a planting site.

The second objective of ReTree is to involve people, especially young people, in planting projects, and at the same time to educate them regarding the importance of trees and forests. Children represent the hope of Earth's forests. It is absolutely critical that we adults indoctrinate children early by word and deed. Nothing can take the place of getting down on your knees in the earth next to a child to help her or him put a tiny seedling in a hole you have dug, packing the earth back around it, then putting a bit of water on the newly turned soil, and after giving the new little seedling your best wishes, going on to the next one.

The third objective of ReTree is to support forestry research. We think that forestry practices must stay abreast of the latest research in genetics, fire and disease control, regeneration, management, and so forth. So ReTree tries to help forestry students in our colleges and universities obtain scholarships, get part-time jobs and housing, and take field trips to nurseries and other institutions.

We collect and distribute seeds needed by scientists in their work. Through the worldwide contacts we have with universities and foresters, we can usually obtain the needed seeds merely by making phone calls.

As part of our scientific experiments with tree plantings, we often supply seeds to government agencies. In one case, I learned that the Forestry Department of Alaska wanted to experiment with a certain species of larch in the interior of the state. It owned a parcel of land near Big Delta, which is about one hundred miles south of Fairbanks on the Alaskan Highway (one of the coldest parts of North America). There, at temperatures as low as seventy below, whatever moisture is in the branches of a tree freezes, and the trees can then explode.

Although the Alaskan State Forestry Department wanted to try the larch, they had no source of seedlings or seeds, so I offered to help get them. I got on the phone and began searching for larch trees or seeds, and found them at the Lawyer Nursery in Plains, Montana. They had thirty thousand seedlings, and were willing to swap them for Sitka spruce seeds. Dr. John Alden of the U.S. Forest Service's research laboratory in Fairbanks had the spruce seeds and was willing to donate them, so the deal was made. Alaska got its larch trees; Lawyer Nursery got several pounds of seeds. Everybody was happy. This is one way that ReTree serves as a seed distributor to scientists around the world. The job fits into our goal of supporting forestry research, and because of my year in the nursery business, I have lots of contacts. Some of them do their work in strange places—like in a mine shaft.

Several years ago, John Blackwell, Director of the World Forestry Center in Portland and a member of ReTree's Board at the time, got a request from someone in Morocco for seedlings that would grow in that country. John asked if I could help find a tree species that might do well in the latitude, elevation, and climate of the proposed planting site, which I think was near Rabat, Morocco's capital.

I contacted the U.S. Forest Service facility located in a place as climatically close as possible to the Moroccan site, in the San Bernardino Mountains of southern California. The people I talked with told me they had some pine seeds they thought would be appropriate, but the seeds would have to be grown into the seedlings needed for the project. Since the seedlings were needed in a hurry, they couldn't be planted in an outdoors nursery; they had to be forced to grow fast.

I scouted around and found a nursery located deep inside an old mine in Kellogg, Idaho. A mine! It seemed weird. But if you think about it, why not? It's warm down there; you can control the humidity and light. Artificially lighting growing areas is no problem, so down in that mine you have a year-round growing season that's completely under control. I contacted the nursery people, who agreed to plant the seeds and grow the seedlings. In just six months or so, I was able to turn over twelve-inch-tall seedlings—all grown in containers in a sterile medium that could pass any agricultural inspection the Moroccan government chose to impose—to John Blackwell.

Now, more than twelve years later, we are trying to organize a tree-planting expedition in Morocco. If it happens, I'm sure going to find out what happened to those pine seedlings.

As part of its effort to help forestry research, ReTree hosts foreign foresters here in Oregon. In 1984 we invited two professional foresters from Taiwan and two from Thailand to visit. We offered to arrange and pay for housing and to conduct them on tours of forests, educational institutions, wood products companies, and other forest related facilities. These visits were very successful. The foresters learned how this country manages its forests, trains its foresters, and conducts research. We, in turn, learned about their techniques, and equally importantly, established relationships we could call on in our overseas projects.

These days, many organizations are interested in reforestation. ReTree was one of the early ones. It is still small, and I suspect it always will be. It still has little financial support other than what I can put into the coffers. At times, it would be easy to become discouraged—there is so much to do and so few resources with which to do it. But if ever I get down and feel sorry for myself, I think of a letter that Dr. Norman Borlaug wrote to me a few years ago.

"Let me congratulate you and your organization for the work which you are doing in tree planting. Your organization, with a very limited budget, is doing more to increase and promote tree planting than many other larger organizations that publish large and complicated scientific treatises on slick paper, but after all is said and done, there are no more trees to show for it. Yours is a straightforward, simple program to encourage young people... to plant trees in many different parts of the world. Most other large promotional programs related to reforestation bewail the disasters of deforestation and do nothing but talk, talk, talk and write, write, write about reforestation, but accomplish very little to show for a large expenditure. Consequently... I again would like to commend you for the effort which you and your organization are making."

My father, E. H. Lockyear (center), with two business associates.
Credit: Lockyear collection

Brothers and sisters (left to right): Dora, Helen, Harold (rear), Ralph (front),
Lula, Fred (rear), Frank (front), Emily, Charles Victor, Mary, William.
Credit: Lockyear collection

Fred York, Scoutmaster of Troop 104,
undoubtedly one of the most influential
people in my early life.
Credit: Lockyear collection

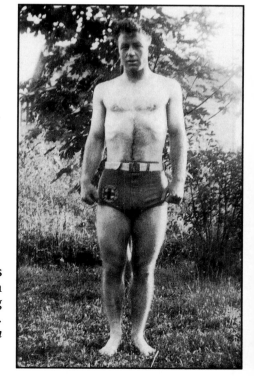

Sixty years younger, sixty pounds
lighter. A newly earned American
Red Cross Senior Lifesaving
patch is on my trunks.
Credit: Lockyear collection

Boy Scout Troop 104. I'm seated,
left front. My lifelong friend,
Allan de Lay, is third from the
left, front row. Ahh, youth.
Credit: Lockyear collection

Eagle Scout Frank Lockyear.
I'd like to have just half this
much hair these days.
Credit: Lockyear collection

My children (left to right)—Richard, Sally, and John—with me in 1954. Both boys earned their Eagle Scout badges. *Credit: Lockyear collection*

Richard's Eagle Scout award ceremony. His grandmother (my mother), aged 89, is at my right. She lived for another twelve years. *Credit: Lockyear collection*

Ralph Hannon (left) and Allan de Lay at our tree planting on Mt. St. Helens, 1986. We have been friends for more than sixty years.
Credit: Lockyear collection

Loren Wheelon, friend from Scouting days. He is with me on many projects, this one in Finland.
Credit: Lockyear collection

Oregon Governor, Vic Atiyeh
(center), and local Scout
Executive, Guy Miller, help me
plant a tree in honor of
Scouting's 75th anniversary.
Guy was an old, old friend. He
died a while back, and we had
a large, memorial tree planting
on Mt. St. Helens that involved
hundreds of Scouts.
Credit: Lockyear collection

Bob Gray prepares
plastic guards to slip over
seedlings as protection from
deer, rabbits, rodents, and other
nibblers. These pesky critters
can cause almost as much
damage as livestock.
Credit: Lockyear collection

A 20-year-old Sitka spruce at King Cove, Alaska. This site at the base of the Aleutian Islands is less than ideal for trees. The same species in a better climate would be 20 to 25 feet tall at this age.
Credit: Lockyear collection

Erosion at Saltillo, Mexico. Local legend says that it was started when Mexican soldiers dug trenches to stop American troops during the war of 1848. I doubt it.
Credit: Lockyear collection

Sitka spruce planted in 1944 on Attu Island in the Aleutians. There was a vicious battle on the island and many American servicemen were killed. The American commander, General Robinson, had these trees brought from the Alaskan mainland and planted in the military cemetery. So far as I know, they are still growing there, one of the few groves of trees on these windswept islands located on the edge of the treeline.
Credit: Allan J. de Lay

Scout Troop #560, Unalaska, Alaska. Even midway out in the Aleutian chain, we still found youngsters eager to help assure forests for the future.
Credit: Lockyear collection

In 1983, a couple of ReTree representatives and I flew to Wrangall, Alaska, to plant trees with the local Girl Scouts. Alaska Helicopters flew us out to Zorumba Island, where we worked in an old clear-cut. Leaders and girls had a great day. Two weeks later I was in Thailand planting trees with 10,000 students.
Credit: Lockyear collection

Father Sergios, pastor of Three Saints at Old Harbor, is one of ReTree's dearest friends. *Credit: Lockyear collection*

Vigdis Finnbogadottir, President of Iceland. Recognizing I would have trouble with her name, I asked if I might address her as "Madam President." *Credit: Lockyear collection*

I take the ReTree message to whatever convention will have me. This one was for Scouts. *Credit: Lockyear collection*

In 1992 we made a swing through the western United States, planting trees with native American tribes. This was in New Mexico, with the Zuni people. *Credit: Lockyear collection*

Tree planting in memory of Robert York, my old Scoutmaster's son. Two visiting foresters from Thailand, plus me and Darci Rivers Pankratz, USFS.
Credit: Allan J. de Lay

On the slopes of Mt. St. Helens, during a memorial planting for my wife, Jean.
Credit: Allan J. de Lay

Planting with Scouts of Troop 379, Longview, Washington, on Mt. St. Helens.
Also (inset) with scoutmaster Denny Bauman in forefront.
Credit: Allan J. de Lay

It isn't every retired nurseryman from Wilsonville, Oregon, who gets to wear a pin of the 101st Airborne. Fort Campbell, 1986. *Credit: Lockyear collection*

In 1989 we planted trees at Patuxent River Naval Air Station in memory of the Challenger Seven crew. With me in the picture (left to right): Captain Donald Wright, the Naval Air Station Commanding Officer; Randy and Becky Resnik; Dr. Charles Resnik, brother of Mission Specialist, Judith Resnik; Jane Smith, widow of shuttle pilot, Michael Smith; Rear Admiral Donald Boecker, Commander of the Naval Air Test Center. *Credit: Lockyear collection*

In 1984 the Boy Scouts of America presented me with the William Hornaday Gold Medallion, Scouting's highest award for work in conservation. Franklin Collins, who was at that time the National Director, came up from headquarters in Texas to make the presentation. *Credit: Allan J. de Lay*

When President Bush came to Portland, I was invited to meet him. I took a few seedlings and a ReTree cap down to the Hilton and gave them to him. *Credit: Photo Art Commercial Studios, Inc.*

These are the people I do it for. It's their future, their planet. We have to pass it on with fertile soil, clean air and water, and a wealth of wildlife. Healthy natural forests can supply them, so I plant forests. *Credit: Lockyear collection*

Chapter 8

Trees grow in forests. If you find trees growing in isolation, odds are they are out there alone because something untoward happened. They were planted by some well-meaning person, or a natural disaster destroyed the others that were there. Or the others were attacked with chain saws, and so only a few, isolated trees that weren't of lumber quality were left.

Trees grow in forests because that is where they are most likely to survive. Their interwoven roots form a powerful collective anchor, and their trunks and branches seem to huddle together against the storms. Trees grow in forests because that is where their seeds fall. When a seed is ripe, it usually falls pretty close to its parent tree. The natural colonization of new territory by trees does not occur in leaps and bounds.

A forest is a community, an exceedingly complex community. Trees are its largest, most majestic citizens, but they are not *the* forest. They share it with many plants and animals.

Animal life abounds in the forest. In my native Pacific Northwest, if you kick apart a decaying log, you'll find it filled with millipedes, wood lice, and springtails. And the forest duff still swarms with billions of microscopic creatures. You'll see deer come to browse on twigs and leaves; maybe hear a coyote or two some moonlit night, working the openings for dinner. There are squirrels and mice and moles. Now and then, a mole loses its way and surfaces, although its feet are totally useless aboveground. Our forests have porcupine, which are pesky creatures that girdle the trees, killing them. We have fox and black bears, too. Not so many as in earlier times, but the bears still come down off the mountains to harvest wild blackberries.

Fungi—among the most ubiquitous of all plant life—pervade the forest. Ranging in size from microscopic yeast to individuals that cover acres of land, they reproduce by spores often housed in specific organs. Their vegetative component consists of microscopic filaments called hyphae, which constitute the mycelium. Fungi don't have chlorophyll, so they cannot manufacture their own food. They feed on other living organisms, or eat dead and decaying organic material. Many fungi are harmful to their hosts, while others are benign.

Of these, fungi which form certain relationships with forest trees are of special importance. Their hyphae encase and invade the trees' roots, establishing a symbiotic relationship called mycorrhiza. The fungi provide the tree with dissolved minerals from the soil, produce growth regulators for the production of new root tips, and raise the host tree's resistance to disease. The tree feeds the fungus with some of the sugars it produces. Mycorrhizal networks pervade the soil of a healthy forest, linking the trees to each other, making them truly intrinsic parts of the whole. A healthy forest cannot exist without mycorrhiza.

A natural forest contains a wealth of other plant life. For example, the tropical rain forest of Costa Rica, which is smaller than West Virginia, contains more than twelve thousand species of plants. The overwhelming majority of forest life resides in the duff and soil of the floor, where countless billions of microscopic creatures exist. In the economy of forest life—of all life for that matter—it would be impossible to overestimate the role played by bacteria. They convert dead organic matter into forms useable by plants and animals; they oxidize nitrites into nitrates and fix atmospheric nitrogen; they are essential in the fermentation process. Microscopic in size, prodigious in population and species, bacteria are in the air, soil, and water, and in the bodies of living and dead animals and plants.

More than eight hundred thousand insect species have been identified and there are probably an equal number still not yet cataloged. Most of them live in the forest, and by and large, are enemies of the trees. They eat leaves and fruit, bore into the wood to lay their eggs, and the larvae open the cambium to invasion by harmful fungi, bacteria, and insects. They lower the resistance to disease of entire stands of trees, opening the way for fungi and bacteria to inflict further damage. In opening large sections of the forest, they increase the danger from wind, and cause an increase in the rate of snow melt and water runoff, thus causing erosion.

Insects can so weaken trees they are considered the worst hazard a forest faces. Yet for all their destruction, insects are essential to the forest. Bees and some moths pollinate many of the forest's flowering plants. Many insects, such as mantis and certain wasps, are death to other insects. Some insects clear away dead wood and help break down detritus, thus releasing minerals back into the earth for reuse. And by opening the forest through destruction, they promote the progression of the forest from the pioneering plants to its climax species.

Worms abound in certain forests. They range in size from tiny roundworms called nematodes—which can weaken trees by attacking the roots and root hairs—to earthworms.

Earthworms are among the most valuable animals of the forest. They aerate the soil with their tunneling and release essential minerals in their castings.

Earthworms aren't common in coniferous forests because of the acidity of the soil. But their populations are fantastic in hardwood forests.

The forest is also home to birds. Here in the Northwest, we have Oregon juncos and jays, red-tailed hawks and golden eagles, great blue herons and water ousels along the rivers.

But as plentiful as life is in our temperate forests, it doesn't hold a candle to that in the tropical rain forest. A typical temperate forest might have four or five species of trees. The same area in a tropical rain forest will have six hundred. The Amazon rain forest has more than five thousand species of trees, more than two-thirds of Earth's four and one-half million species of plants, and one-tenth of all bird species. There are more orchids there than any other place on Earth, as well as twenty-five-foot tall violets. The insect count is beyond measure. Forty-three species of ants were counted on *one* tree in the Amazonian rain forest. Yet, with it all, scientists believe that fewer than one-third of the animal and plant species living in the Amazon rain forest have been found. At the rate it's being destroyed, they might never be found.

The world's forests cover about one-third of the planet's land surface—roughly twelve billion acres. At one time, they represented one-quarter of the land, and covered regions where they are in short supply today—the Near East, the Mediterranean littoral, and Western Europe. They girdled the globe along the equator and blanketed the eastern half of North America from the Gulf of Mexico to the Canadian shield.

I can't get all that land reforested, but I'm trying.

Chapter 9

On August 14, 1933, a fire flared up in the tinder-dry forests of Gales Creek Canyon, Oregon. The Tillamook fire, as it is called, burned for twenty days, engulfed 290,000 acres, and destroyed twelve billion board feet of timber. Ash from the Tillamook burn fell on ships five hundred miles out to sea.

Wildfires are among the most serious dangers a forest faces. They are caused by nature and humans—lightning and carelessness.

There are three kinds of wildfires: surface, crown, and ground. Surface fires burn the litter and small plants, including many tree seedlings. Crown fires burn in the canopy, and are driven by high winds. They can burn so hot that they generate their own fire storms. Ground fires occur in the forest duff, and can burn for months. Of the three types, crown fires are the most destructive and difficult to control.

About eight million lightning bolts strike the Earth each day. A lightning bolt generates temperatures of close to twenty-one thousand degrees Fahrenheit. Most wood ignites at 750 degrees. A large number of lightning bolts hit trees, and about seventy percent of them cause fires. If lightning is accompanied by rain, the blaze usually is extinguished in minutes, but dry lightning is bad.

Theodore Roosevelt established the U.S. Forest Service in 1905, and one of its mandates was fire control. The nation's first head of the USFS, Gifford Pinchot, wrote that, "…(T)he question of forest fires may be shelved for some time, at enormous cost in the end, but sooner or later it must be met."

Worldwide, wildfires cause great destruction and loss of life. In 1894 a fire near Hinckley, Minnesota, destroyed five towns and killed more than four hundred people. The Peshtigo, Wisconsin, fire in 1871 killed fifteen hundred people. In 1902, there were more than 110 wildfires in Oregon and Washington. Three million acres of Montana and Idaho forests were destroyed and eighty-five firefighters killed in a 1910 fire. In 1987 a careless worker pouring gas into his chain saw started a fire that burned four million acres of forest along the China/Soviet Union border.

Fire detection is critical to fire control. Early in the Forest Service's fire control efforts, lookouts plotted the fires on topographic maps so that the crews could reach them in the shortest time. There is a photo in the book, *100 Years of Federal Forestry*, published by the U.S. Forest Service, of a ranger patrolling his area in a Model T Ford, converted to ride railroad tracks. Over the years, lookout towers were built on mountain peaks. At first they were simple platforms built in the tops of tall trees, just a place to stand. In their evolution, the towers developed into sturdy, one-room shelters, often thirty or forty feet off the ground on spidery towers. The towers were networked to each other and to ranger stations by telephone, and later by radio. From their beginnings, lookout towers were often staffed by young men and women, often college students, who spent the entire fire season alone in their isolated towers searching the horizon for telltale smoke.

I guess life in one of those towers could get lonely at times. But at other times, it must be pretty exciting. I met a young man who had spent several summers in a tower in northern California, and he said that the most exciting times were during electrical storms. I can just imagine! There he was, in a steel tower set on top of a mountain— the largest lightning rod around. He said he put the legs of his stool in water glasses to insulate it, then climbed into the seat and sweated out the experience.

In 1921 the Forest Service initiated a blimp fire patrol, and today fixed-wing aircraft and helicopters have replaced almost all the lookouts.

Early in the history of the Forest Service, the fighting of wildfires was pretty crude. Those early firefighters' equipment consisted of shovels, buckets for water, pieces of burlap for smothering the flames, and strong backs to handle the gear. Today, highly trained teams of firefighters have a wide range of tools, from chain saws to bulldozers and aerial tankers, at their disposal. Over the years, one of the most dramatic firefighting techniques uses smoke jumpers, who parachute from planes to fight small, isolated fires until the larger ground crews can reach the site. The Forest Service experimented with smoke jumping beginning in 1938 in Washington, and today there are hundreds of qualified men and women on call during the fire season.

I was the assistant Scoutmaster of Troop 104 when the Tillamook fire happened. When the call went out that Boy Scouts were needed to help reforest the burn, we were prepared. We all climbed into my car and drove out to the burn and spent a couple of hours or so planting trees. Planting the Tillamook burn became so popular, and so many Oregonians came out to help, that the State Forestry Department had to organize the project. They established areas along the highway where volunteers could park for the day. Foresters would meet the parties, escort them to planting areas, demonstrate proper techniques, then bring the people back to their cars at the end of the day. Three hundred eleven thousand acres of land is a lot of real estate, and in the Coast Range, it would be easy for someone to get lost, even though all the tree cover had been burned off.

The Tillamook burn reforestation project was a massive effort, and if there had to be such a destructive fire, it couldn't have been in a better place for successful regeneration. The Coast Range has good soil, which was enriched even further by organic material left by the fire. There is a good, reliable supply of precipitation, and the plantings were made early each year when conditions were optimal.

What had been a barren moonscape right after the fire is now completely covered by trees. The plantings took place in the late 1930s and early fifties, and the first logging of those second-growth trees began a couple of years ago.

Mt. St. Helens is in the Gifford Pinchot National Forest, a place I know well. During my active days with Troop 104, I took the Scouts up there many times on tree-planting expeditions and for high adventure. We made many climbs of the mountain, which is considered the most beautiful volcanic peak in the country, if not the world.

The eruption of Mt. St. Helens on May 18, 1980, tore sixteen hundred feet off the top of the peak and spewed more than half a cubic mile of ash and dust into the air. Sixty people were killed and tens of thousands of magnificent trees bowled over like tenpins.

I organized the first experimental tree planting on the mountain after the eruption and, thanks to the active cooperation of the Forest Service, went up into the Red Zone with a troop of Scouts. Because this area was closed to the general public, we had to travel in a convoy under the control of the Forest Service, with rangers Rocky Pancrantz and Darci Rivers riding shotgun.

A couple of years later, Rocky and Darci were married. Darci has gone with ReTree representatives to tree plantings in Alaska and Mexico.

The Mt. St. Helens' planting site is a high promontory called Deadman's Ridge. Just one canyon separates it from the peak of Mt. St. Helens, so we had a good view of the devastation caused by the eruption. There seemed to be nothing, absolutely nothing left alive. The landscape was the dull gray of the ash and pumice the volcano threw out, and there seemed to be not one bird, mammal, or sprig of greenery as far as we could see. But if you got down close to the ground, you could see tiny plants returning, and rodent tracks. The Forest Service's wildlife manager told me that even some large mammals could be seen now and then, wending their way across the barren hillsides.

Of course we shouldn't be surprised that Mt. St. Helens is regenerating itself. It has probably erupted countless times over the past million years or so. It's just that, for all but a few thousand of those years, there were no people around to see what was happening. Natural disasters heal themselves, given enough time.

The natural regeneration of a forest can take many years, even centuries, depending on several factors, like climate, temperature, precipitation, soil type, and topography. Our Pacific Northwest forests tend to return relatively fast because the conditions for regrowth are so favorable. So a human can actually witness regrowth in his lifetime.

The first life to return to a coniferous forest in the Northwest after a natural disaster, and even after some instances of human activity, are fungi and bacteria. There are "good" and "bad" kinds of each. Some fungi cause disease in plants and animals; some kinds are essential for the health of a forest. Some bacteria will kill their host; others are important in the conversion of chemicals into useable nutrients.

The first plants to colonize a devastated area of forest are the grasses, sedges, and so forth. These herbaceous plants need sunlight, so thrive in the areas opened by wildfire. They begin the process of building soil destroyed by fire, water, volcanic activity, and other processes that destroy, wash away, or cover the former topsoil.

After a few years, the clearing is invaded by bushes, the first of the woody plants. In the Northwest, one of the important invaders is the red alder. This member of the birch family has nodules on its roots that fix nitrogen in the soil, converting it into a form that can be used by the tree and other plants for nutrition. The "bush" period in the regeneration of a coniferous forest might last for more than twenty years. Eventually, all things being equal, these sun-loving woody plants give way to the original species, the firs, hemlocks, and cedars. In the moist western parts of the Northwest, the first of these is apt to be the Douglas fir. Its seeds will blow in on the wind, be carried in on the fur of animals, and be scattered by birds and rodents. Those that land on favorable soil and escape being eaten, frozen, dried out in scorching summers, or washed away in floods, or countless other hazards, will germinate and sprout. If the seedlings survive—and most of them will not—eventually they will shade out the deciduous alders and other woody plants and once more become the dominant species in that part of the forest.

A few years ago, I revisited Deadman's Ridge and was pleased to see how well the little trees we planted are doing.

Recently, I lost a dear Scouting friend, Guy Miller, a former Scout executive, and one of the people who helped me start ReTree. A few years ago, he was appointed to coordinate local Scouting's tree planting. We had known each other since we were kids.

Well, Guy died recently after surgery. We are planning a very large memorial tree planting with the Scouts for the spring of 1993. The Forest Service has made a site up on Mt. St. Helens available for the planting, and with the help of the local Scout Councils we should get hundreds of boys and their leaders to participate. It could be the largest event of its kind on the mountain since it erupted.

ReTree has conducted commemorative tree plantings of this kind for several years. They seem to be a nice way to honor special people or remember certain events. And they help put a few more trees back into the earth.

The first one ReTree was involved in took place at Fort Campbell, Kentucky. My friend Alvin Foleen called me one day and said he had seen a news item on TV about a young girl in Toronto, Canada. She wanted to plant some trees in memory of the American servicemen of the 101st Airborne Division who were killed in an airline crash at Gander, Newfoundland, in December, 1985. Alvin thought this might be a project in which we could help, and I agreed. The following day I called the Gander Chamber of Commerce, the local newspapers, and the police, to learn the girl's name. The police suggested another person to contact. He was a school principal who, although he didn't know any more than the others, got quite interested when I explained who we were. He said, "Give me a few days. Maybe I can be of some help." About a week later, he called back with the girl's name, address, and phone number, and I got in touch with Janice Johnson and her family. She seemed to be a nice person, fourteen years old, and deeply touched by the tragedy that had come upon so many American families. I explained that ReTree International didn't want to intrude, but if we could be of help in her project, we were available. She said that she didn't know where to plant the trees or where to get them, or how to organize the project. At that point, she was just trying to get contributions. When I explained what ReTree is and does, she and her family eagerly invited our help.

I suggested that Fort Campbell, Kentucky, the home base of the 101st Airborne, might be the logical place to plant the trees. Janice agreed. I contacted the commanding officer, Major General Burton D. Patrick, who was very enthusiastic about the idea, and offered base personnel to help. I recalled meeting some nurserymen from Canada at a convention some years earlier and I got on the phone and talked with them. They suggested that Canadian maple might be an appropriate species to plant, and offered to contribute both the trees and the transportation for them to Fort Campbell. Because there were still some expenses, I phoned one of ReTree's best friends, Harry Merlo, President of Louisiana-Pacific Corporation. He helped, as he so often does.

So, in September of 1986, I stood beside a fine young girl who had wanted to do something in memory of servicemen from a friendly neighboring nation. There were 248 trees planted at Fort Campbell that day, one for each of the dead soldiers.

ReTree has had excellent cooperation with all the branches of the military. They have been partners in many of our tree plantings, offering sites for the seedling trees, manpower to help plant them, transportation, and refreshments—whatever they can legally and conveniently do to help.

Emily Mead:

As the director of the Office of Special Events in the Bush White House, I met Frank at the Patuxent Naval Air Station. He had a tree planting there to commemorate the crew of Challenger 7. The ceremony was at eleven o'clock, and the children were there and each one was assigned to a Navy man. Each man took his little student out and they planted trees in pre-dug holes. They did the whole thing in about twenty minutes. Planted two thousand trees. A very lovely and caring time. I think everybody felt sort of warm, sort of a warm, fuzzy feeling.

For many years I had hoped to do something to commemorate the American servicemen and -women killed in the Vietnam war. The obvious thing would be to plant forest trees, so that is what I proposed to several veterans groups and service clubs. They all thought it was a great idea until the price tag was mentioned. Gradually the idea slipped to the back burner as I got more and more busy with projects that could be done.

One of them was the planting of a forest by and for the Lions clubs in Oregon. I talked with Bill Rollins, the District Governor of Lions International, about it. He liked the idea, so I contacted the U.S. Forest Service to find a site. They had thirteen idle acres in the Mount Hood National Forest up near the Collowash River. How much would it cost to plant that much land to trees, we asked? Twenty-five hundred dollars, was the answer.

To raise interest in the project, Bill and I invited a few key Lions from around the state to a tree planting at the site. It was just a token plant, no more than a hundred trees, but it gave the people an idea of what we had in mind.

The next challenge was money, and Bill and I set out to collect it from Lions clubs around Oregon. My club, the Wilsonville Lions, contributed five hundred dollars. Another club matched that sum. We raised two thousand dollars, and the Forest Service said that this was enough, that the planting wouldn't cost as much as they had originally estimated.

Contributions to the Lions Forest continued to trickle in well after all the trees were planted, and I suggested to Bill Rollins that it go toward the Lions participation in a Vietnam memorial forest. At last it seemed that my old dream might actually come true. Bill and I approached several Lions clubs around the state and were met with enthusiasm for the project.

To find a site, or sites, we went to the Oregon State Department of Forestry. The state owns large tracts of land on which it plants trees. Jim Brown, the State Forester, thought the concept of a forest dedicated to the Americans killed in Vietnam was an excellent idea. He agreed to find the land, which would have to be quite large to accommodate the number of trees we had in mind. Our goal was to plant one tree for each of the 58,130 servicemen and women lost in Vietnam. We suggested that the trees be planted in four areas within the state, matching the four Lions districts.

As in the case of the Lions Forest, we decided to have the trees planted professionally. That meant more fund-raising.

Bill Rollins and I hit the road again.

It went reasonably well, but coming on the heels of the Lions Forest solicitation, the dollars were fewer than before. We needed a new approach.

I had organized and conducted plant sales with the Scouts, and knew such events could raise money. So I got a group of local Lions together to organize one. A local supermarket donated the use of a corner of its parking lot, and several truckloads of plants were contributed by nurseries. That first weekend we made twenty-three hundred dollars, then another thousand the following weekend. A Lions club in Eugene raised still another one thousand dollars. To date we have raised about eight thousand dollars.

On April 11, 1992, we dedicated the forest at a rest stop on a highway west of Portland. ReTree representatives, a delegation of Lions, color guards from the Vietnam Veterans Association, and officials of the State Forestry

Department participated. It was quite an event.

During the plant sale, a Vietnam veteran, Ed O'Keefe, came up to the table and introduced himself. He was an officer in the local Vietnam Veterans Association, and as he learned more about the project, indicated that the organization probably would be interested in participating. Now we had ReTree, the Lions, and the veterans.

The Lions established a committee to organize and coordinate the Vietnam project—"Lions Say Yes for Trees." It has become a permanent committee to continue promoting tree planting in the Lions club when the Vietnam forest is finished.

Chapter 10

Born in 1798, David Douglas was a noted Scottish horticulturist. During his brief career, he collected thousands of plants. The more significant of them he mounted on collection sheets along with their twigs, flowers, seeds, and so forth, plus a detailed sketch if the plant were a large one, such as a bush or tree. Many of Douglas' collections can still be seen in herbaria, especially in England.

As a young man, he came to the attention of William Jackson Hooker, professor of botany at Glasgow University. Hooker described Douglas as possessed of "...great activity, undaunted courage, singular abstemiousness and energetic zeal." In 1823, possibly because of Hooker's recommendation, Douglas was sent to the United States by the prestigious Horticultural Society to buy fruit trees in New York state and Canada and see to their shipment back to England. In his spare time, he was to collect native flora. In a display of his energetic zeal, Douglas developed the skill of shooting fruit, leaves, and cones from high in the trees, a method of collecting which he used for the rest of his life.

Douglas lacked the scientific and academic background to be considered a trained, professional botanist; his dedication to the science was as a practical explorer and collector. In this role he was eminently successful. He introduced California poppies, lupines, penstemons, evening primrose, and many other decorative plants to England. Of the seventeen pines native to the western United States, Douglas discovered seven. In the more than 150 years since his death, he has had his name *(Douglassi* or *Douglasiana*), attached to eighty-six species or varieties of plants—more than any other person.

In 1824, when Douglas was just twenty-three years old, the Hudson's Bay Company sent him to it's post at Fort Vancouver in the Pacific Northwest to collect plants. Because no biologist accompanied him, he was also directed to collect animals when possible. En route, his ship traveled down the Atlantic seaboard of North and South America, through the infamous Straits of Magellan and up the Pacific. It put in briefly at the island of Mas-a-Tierra, where Alexander Selkirk, the character on which Robinson Crusoe was based, was marooned for more than four years.

Fort Vancouver was on the Columbia River at its confluence with the Willamette. The river had been discovered by white men thirty-two years earlier. Since Magellan entered the Pacific in 1517, three or four explorers had sailed past its mouth without realizing that the major river of that corner of the continent lay just beyond the bar. George Vancouver suspected this because of the fresh water found in the ocean four miles offshore. But a storm kept him from exploring the possibility, and when he finally got around to testing his suspicion, he was too late. Captain Robert Gray of Boston sailed over the bar at the river's mouth on May 11, 1792. After proceeding a few miles upstream, he anchored and explored the surrounding countryside. Before leaving, he noted the river on his chart, and named it for his ship, the Columbia. Vancouver came upriver later in the year, and claimed the land in the name of George III of England.

David Douglas arrived at Fort Vancouver when the settlement was the hub of the Hudson's Bay Company's beaver trapping enterprises in the Northwest. Tens of thousands of the animals were trapped and their pelts sent back to England to satisfy an insatiable appetite for beaver hats. Still more were killed to reduce the population in an effort to thwart American trappers, who were intruding into this English fiefdom. Patriotism had little, if anything, to do with the company's actions.

They simply wanted to protect their profits.

Douglas collected extensively along the Pacific coast. He discovered a pine tree with bark cracked like an alligator's hide—*Pinus pondrose.* The Northwest's ponderosa pine is a major timber tree to this day. One of the first plants he encountered still bears his name, Douglas fir, (*Pseudotsuga menziessi*). The horticulturist was overwhelmed by this tree. "Those in... forests arrive at a magnitude exceeded by few if any trees in the world. One felled tree was 227 feet long, and more than forty-eight feet in circumference—more than fifteen feet in diameter." This tree is the basis for the timber industry in the Pacific Northwest. Doug Fir, as it's called hereabout, constitutes eighty-five percent of the coniferous trees in the Pacific Northwest. I doubt that any of those giants that Douglas saw still exist.

Douglas traveled upstream on the Columbia doing his botanizing. The Indians called him the "Grass Man" because of his interest in plants, and figured he was crazy. When he told them he was collecting for his king, George III—which was not quite true—they assumed the king was crazy to send someone halfway around the world just to pick plants.

One of the plants Douglas collected was the camas, a wild hyacinth which the Indians dug up to eat its tuber. Douglas tried it and said it tasted pleasant, like baked pears. He avoided eating the tuber however, because it caused flatulence. He wrote that once, while sleeping in an Indian lodge, he "...was almost blown out by the strength of the wind."

In traveling up the river, Douglas passed through the Gorge, a deep gash the river has carved through the Cascades. He climbed the cliffs on the south side, a place of "towering rock precipices, the delicate lace of waterfalls tumbling a sheer one hundred feet or more, towers, castles and pinnacles in the colored rock." Today the Gorge is a National Scenic Area.

Douglas met and lived among many of the Indian tribes of the Northwest. If one can read between the lines of his journals, he fell in love with the princess of a Chinook group, and probably had a baby by her. He visited her village a couple of times afterward, but didn't acknowledge the child, so the facts in the matter are obscure. However, there is reason to believe that his "singular abstemiousness" did not extend to matters of the heart.

Douglas returned to England, then made a second trip to the New World, during which he botanized down the Pacific coastline as far as Santa Barbara. (California was then still Mexican territory.) Near Santa Cruz, he saw the Giant sequoia, *Sequoia sempervirens,* for the first time. He couldn't believe that such trees existed. "I have measured them frequently 275 feet long, and thirty-two feet around three feet from the ground. Some I saw were upward of three hundred feet long." He sent the almost microscopically tiny seeds back home, thus introducing *Sempervirens* to England, where they are relatively common today.

A few years ago, while in Lockersbie, Scotland, trying to arrange a commemorative tree planting honoring Pan American's Flight 103 victims, I saw an enormous Giant sequoia growing in the village.

In Santa Barbara, Douglas mixed his botanizing with a bit of hands-on biologizing. "The ladies are handsome, of a dark olive brunette, with good teeth, and dark fine eyes, which bespeaks the descendants of Castille, Catalonia or Leon. They have a greater recommendation than personal attractions. They are very amiable." The horticulturist would have been a good catch, a man of science and emissary of the famous Horticultural Society. Had he been snared, given the fecundity of these dark-eyed beauties, he probably would have contributed to what was an exploding population in California. Families of fifteen, twenty, and even more children were more the norm than exception. As one commentator noted, "The loaves were no sooner out of the oven than a fresh batch was warming up."

But Douglas wasn't about to be caught. He had planned

to botanize all the way to the Mexican border, but when the authorities forbade this he headed back to Fort Vancouver.

In 1832 he visited what would one day become British Columbia, and attempted a trip down the Fraser River, a singularly foolish thing to do. The canoe overturned, Douglas almost drowned, and he lost all his botanical notes and specimens, and his personal journal. Despondent over the turn of events within the Horticultural Society, which had recently fired his boss, Douglas resigned and in the winter of 1833 took ship for Hawaii.

He landed in Fairhaven (Honolulu) where he collected and mounted more than two thousand fern specimens which he forwarded to England. He traveled to the big island—Hawaii—where he camped at the edge of Kilauea, "...a fiery lake, roaring and boiling in fearful majesty."

In July, Douglas sailed back to the big island in the company of an amateur geologist, the Reverend John Diell, his family, and the family servant, John. Douglas grew bored with the journey and left the ship at Kohala Point with John and a dog named Billy, who had been the horticulturist's companion for years. His intention was to hike Mauna Kea, the island's 13,784 foot high peak and rejoin the Diells in the town of Hilo.

John wasn't much of a hiker apparently, since Douglas left him at the hut of one of the cattle hunters they encountered, and he was never seen again. The third day out, Douglas met Edward Gurney, another cattle hunter, who cautioned Douglas about the cattle pits on the slopes of Mauna Kea. The hunters dug these holes to trap the wild cattle—descendants of animals turned loose by early whalers as a source of fresh beef that abounded on the island. Gurney accompanied Douglas a few miles on the mountain, then was sent back by the impatient horticulturist because of his slow pace. The following morning, a group of natives told Gurney that something had happened, and led him to one of the cattle pits. In the bottom of the pit, a bull was trapped and a piece of cloth poked from the mud under his hooves. Gurney shot the animal, and with the natives' help, dragged a body out. It was that of thirty-five-year-old David Douglas. Nearby the little dog, Billy, was found guarding the pack Douglas had been carrying the last time Gurney saw him.

Douglas' body was taken to Honolulu where an autopsy indicated the possibility that the horticulturist had been murdered. When Douglas had parted company with Gurney, he had been carrying a large sum of money. It was missing, so the motive could have been robbery; or Douglas might have been collecting something cozier than plants. Gurney, who was known to be a violent man, had a common-law wife, a native Hawaiian who was said to be very attractive.

In the late 1980s, ReTree traveled to Hawaii to help plant trees at the site of the David Douglas monument five thousand feet above sea level on the slopes of Mauna Kea. The monument is a simple stone shaft set in a small grove of *Pseuotsuga menziesii* that were planted a generation ago, also in remembrance.

Douglas' body is not there, however. It was buried in a small churchyard in Honolulu, in the native section. Over the years the site has reverted to grass and bushes, and whatever marker placed there has disappeared.

Chapter 11

One of our goals is to plant trees wherever they can grow, and our most northern state certainly tests that goal. So Alaska has been a great testing ground for ReTree. We have planted trees in just about every part of Alaska ranging from the southeastern panhandle to the interior near Fairbanks, to the outer Aleutian Islands, to the shore of the Bering Sea. Not all of those areas might seem conducive to tree growth, and maybe they aren't. But Alaska gives us a superb laboratory to find out.

After our initial tree planting to commemorate the state's twenty-fifth anniversary, we conducted many projects in Alaska. Some were designed especially for young people, like the one in the early 1980s. There, in the delightful company of about fifteen Girl Scouts, we flew by helicopter out to Zarembo Island and planted a few Sitka spruce seedlings.

For several years, I had been interested in determining if the Aleutians, which once were forested and which still have about the same climate as before the Ice Ages, would support trees. There are several factors working against this. The islands suffer terrific winds—an Aleutian williwaw can peel your skin off. Also the soil was 'dozed off time after time by the Ice Age glaciers, leaving most of it thin and deficient in the nutrients trees need. Although the island chain has the Japanese current to moderate its temperature fluctuations, the growing season is very short. But maybe, in some of the sheltered sites out of the wind, near streams, with some humus buildup over the mineral soil, trees just might grow. I wanted to find out.

Realizing that I needed more information about cold

climate silviculture, I visited the U.S. Forest Service's Northwest Range and Experiment Station in Portland. There I met David Bruce, a retired Forest Service employee who was still active with the programs underway at the station. When I explained my interest in the Aleutians, David suggested I get in touch with Dr. John Alden, a tree geneticist, a graduate of the Forestry Department of Oregon State University, and the best friend ReTree has in Alaska. Currently he is stationed in Fairbanks with the agency's Northern Forestry Institute. When I mentioned my interest in experimental plantings, he suggested doing one at Unalaska in the Aleutians.

The Aleutian archipelago stretches like a curved sword about twelve hundred miles westward from the Alaskan Peninsula toward Asia. At one time it was part of Beringia, the strip of land that joined Asia to North America during the Ice Ages. The Aleutians form a transition zone between the Bering Sea and the Pacific. Fossil wood from trees related to today's metasequoia, the so-called dawn redwood, and from hardwoods dating back several million years, have been found on several of the islands. Tree stumps more than forty thousand years old have been uncovered, and petrified bits of trees have been found on Unalaska. I have a small fragment of petrified tree taken from Unga Island near Sand Point, so I know that, over geological ages, the Aleutians have supported forests. Since the retreat of the last Ice Age, the only trees of any significance have been those planted by humans.

The first trees planted in North America for human use as lumber and for fuel were put in the ground by Russians on Unalaska Island. Because there are thick forests in other parts of Alaska with climates comparable to the Aleutians, the absence of trees on the islands is a mystery. Some scientists suspect that the absence of certain species, such as Sitka spruce, can be blamed on the area's wet weather. Spruce need fairly dry days for the seeds to mature, and there are precious few dry days in the Aleutians.

The Russians were the first white men to colonize

Alaska. The first of them, led by the Danish-Russian explorer, Vitus Bering, came with a charge from Peter the Great to determine whether Asia was connected to America. At one time it was, but Bering missed it by about ten thousand years. Beringia was inundated when the last of the Ice Ages passed.

While it existed, Berengia was a bridge between Asia and America. Each of these have animal species that initially were alien to the other, so we know traffic headed both east and west across Berengia. The camel and horse, for example, originated in America. During the Ice Ages both of them crossed over the bridge into Asia. The horse became extinct in the western hemisphere and didn't reappear until the Spaniards reintroduced it in the sixteenth century. The camels that stayed in the New World evolved into guanacos and llamas. Those in Asia evolved into dromedaries with one hump and bactrians with two humps. The tapir originated in North America and crossed into Asia. Today there are two species, one in Central America, and another in Southeastern Asia. Moose crossed over the Berengia land bridge into America, as did bison and elk. They still exist on the Eurasian land mass, but are slightly different than their American relatives.

When game animals crossed into North America from Asia, human hunters followed. Exactly when these first immigrants arrived we don't know. Archeological evidence is inconclusive, but the accepted dates go back as far as fifteen thousand years ago. Some experts argue that human occupation of the Western Hemisphere dates back far earlier, perhaps to forty-five thousand years ago. Whenever they came, these early Americans took advantage of the ice-free land of Berengia. Their passage deeper into the continent was made possible by an open corridor between the Cordelarian ice sheet that covered much of the western part of the continent and the Laurentian to the east. The people were funneled, as it were, south, onto the warm, lush grasslands in the continent's interior, with its wealth of game animals and plant life. In my opinion, some of those people who passed through, or stayed in what is now western Alaska, consumed all the trees growing there. The trees have not come back, and unless there is human intervention, it is unlikely they will regenerate for a long, long time.

So, although Titus Bering was too late to see a land bridge between Asia and America, he did discover the land that would be known for more than a century as Russian Alaska.

Bering died of scurvy during his second voyage, and the survivors of the expedition returned to Siberia with sea otter pelts they had bought or stolen from the native population.

The otter's incredibly beautiful, soft fur was instantly in demand throughout Europe, and a horde of fur traders swooped down on Alaska. They enslaved the Aleuts, pressing them into service as otter hunters, and in the process of the enslavement, almost eliminated them. Tuberculosis, syphilis, and measles, plus the imposition of extremely harsh living conditions reduced the Aleut population from about twenty-five thousand to roughly three thousand. As sea otter hunters, the Aleuts were singularly successful. By the time the United States bought Alaska in 1867, the animal was all but extinct from the outer Aleutians to California.

In 1805, under orders from the Russian Chamberlain of Alaska, Nicolai Petrovich Rezanov, Sitka spruce seedlings were brought from the forests at Sitka and planted at the village of Unalaska on Amaknak Island. Twenty-six years later, a Russian Orthodox priest, Father Veniaminov, reported that twenty-four of the trees were still alive and had grown to about eight and one-half feet tall and five and one-half inches in diameter. In 1899, a professional forester named Bernard Fernow discovered that two groups of trees, one of twelve and another of seven trees, had survived. The largest of the trees were twenty-five to thirty feet tall, with diameters of two feet. By 1943, there were only thirteen trees left, the others having been destroyed during military construction projects.

My brother was at the naval base near Dutch Harbor during World War II. He told me about a group of spruce trees growing on Unalaska Island that were supposed to be more than one hundred years old. Some of them had to be the original Rezanov planting. I was intrigued to know that the Aleutians could support at least some species, and I was determined to find out which ones. When ReTree visited Unalaska in May 1987, six of the trees planted in 1805 were still living, and there were more than one thousand seedlings, some two feet tall, from seeds produced by the parent trees. Perhaps the seeds from which they sprouted had come to maturity in a relatively dry period. That grove of trees, called the Sitka Spruce Plantation, is a national historic landmark— the only trees in the United States so designated.

In addition to the spruce on Amaknak Island, there are a few other groves on the Aleutians, all of them planted by humans, and many the work of American servicemen stationed on the islands during the Second World War. In 1944, General Simon B. Bruckner decided that, as a morale booster, systematic tree planting should be undertaken on the islands, and Adak has its own national forest with a marker in front of the tiny grove to prove it.

Much of the information I have noted here about past tree plantings in the Aleutians comes from David Bruce's notes and scientific papers. David was in the Aleutians during World War II, and was assigned to the tree planting project to observe older planting sites, select new ones, and take soil samples.

There has been no regeneration of the forests that existed on the Aleutians before the Ice Ages, unless we stretch a point and grant the seedlings spawned by the Rezenov spruce trees on Amaknak that distinction. If the earth warms and dries from the greenhouse effect, natural regeneration could happen. But it will be a slow process. On Kodiak Island, for example, which has a much more beneficent climate than the islands farther west, the rate of forest regeneration is roughly one mile per century!

In addition to the trees growing at Sitka Spruce

Plantation, there is another, much younger group—planted this century—of Sitka spruce growing on Unalaska Island near the UniSea Corporation's seafood processing plant. When I first saw the spruce, the fumes from the plant's stack were blowing among the trees and appeared to be damaging them. So a few years after our first tree planting at Unalaska, I contacted the corporate headquarters and discussed the situation with officials there. When they learned what was happening at their facility, they were most concerned and agreed to cooperate in remedying the situation. ReTree obtained seedlings and a group of the corporation's employees helped plant them.

Our relationships with businesses generally give us reason for optimism. Almost without exception, when we have approached the private sector with information about questionable practices or requests for help, we have been met with positive, friendly responses. Even when the practices are not changed and the requests denied, there has seldom been any confrontational relationship. Since ReTree is a very small organization, totally dependent on grants and contributions for support, a significant number of which come from corporations, this is wonderful.

In all of our projects in Alaska, we have been blessed by good corporate friends. Each time we have gone north, Alaska Airlines, E.K.A. Air, Mark Air, Reeves Aleutian Airlines, and Peninsula Air have been there with assistance. Generosity like this has been more the rule than the exception throughout the airline industry. Pan American took us to Europe several times, as did Scandinavian Airways. So, when I appeared with my hand out, we were hauled, bag and baggage, to the city of Kodiak. From there we would fly to Old Harbor, courtesy of Father Sergios, a Greek Orthodox priest.

Because the Piper Apache we took from Kodiak to Old Harbor was on a commercial run and subject to FAA regulations, the crew had to make the usual announcements about seat belts, and so forth. The crew consisted of a flight-jacketed, blue-jeaned, boondockerbooted pilot. At the downwind end of the runway, he shouted back over his shoulder, "This is a 'no smoking' flight. So if you want to light up, you'll have to step outside." As we skirted the mountains towering above us, he suggested that we look for bears on the grassy slopes, since Kodiak Island is home of the great brown bear, the largest carnivore on earth. These bears can grow to be more than nine feet long, and weigh up to three-quarters of a ton. According to most reports, they don't attack humans unless attacked or unless their young are in danger. This is an interesting hypothesis that I for one don't care to test. We didn't see any bears on the way into Old Harbor, but were told by the people there that an old boar—a male bear—was hanging around the area.

Flying into Old Harbor is quite an experience. The village is crowded between a very impressive mountain on one side and Sitalidak Strait on the other. The gravel landing strip is parallel to, and just a few feet from, the town's one and only street, which is also a gravel strip. We buzzed the strip, flew out over the water, hung a hard left, and plunked down. One of the party asked the pilot how many times he had come into Old Harbor. "That landing was a tad over the two thousandth one," came his response.

When we crawled out of the Piper Apache, Father Sergios was standing at the head of a small group of people. Black-robed, black-hatted, and veiled, he also wore boondockers. His arms were spread as though in benediction, and a gleaming smile was sandwiched between a black mustache and long, black beard. His robes looked as though they had just come off the ironing board, and even the Apache's prop wash didn't so much ruffle as swirl them in well-ordered patterns around his body. In all the days we were in Old Harbor, I never saw him dressed otherwise, whether hosting us at meals, showing off his tiny church, driving a pickup, or on the end of a shovel digging holes for the trees.

We followed Father Sergios through Old Harbor—not too much of a hike—to the rectory next to the tiny church at the edge of town. My memories of Father Sergios always include following him—along the muddy street of Old Harbor, through the crazy traffic of downtown Thesaloniki, Greece, into and out of airports in northern Greece, onto city busses, off the buses, wherever we went together.

Most of the houses in Old Harbor were built at the same time from one set of blueprints. A basic gabled-roof rectangle, each house achieves its modicum of individuality from paint—primary red, yellow, and blue. The church is the same basic rectangle shape, a bit enlarged, and is white with a blue roof, topped by three blue, onion-shaped domes, each crowned by a white, three-barred Russian cross.

The original village, located on Three Saints Bay, one headland removed from the present site, was the first permanent Russian settlement and continuous Orthodox Christian community in Alaska. It was wiped out by a flood and rebuilt a few miles east on the northern shore of Sitkalidak Strait.

At the rectory Father Sergios, leading by example, asked that we remove our shoes before entering. I thought this might have some religious significance, but as we stepped inside I discovered why no shoes were allowed. The interior of that plain wooden house in Old Harbor looked as if it had been lifted out of a museum. A walnut dining table was covered by a lace cloth, and illuminated by a crystal chandelier. Old, velvet upholstered chairs and an antique sideboard sat on deep-piled carpeting. Family heirlooms abounded.

"Now we'll have a bite to eat, then I'll show you your accommodations."

Since Father Sergios does not eat red meat, we existed on salmon. Old Harbor is a fishing village, and it was salmon season. We had the freshest, most delicious salmon I have ever eaten, and in all those meals, it was never prepared in the same way twice. It came whole and baked, filleted and broiled, poached, and accompanied by mouth-watering side dishes like hard-boiled eggs, potatoes, and fresh vegetables, all cooked to perfection. Heavy, black bread came from his own oven, and was served with delicate, aromatic teas or black coffee. There in Old Harbor, Alaska, sandwiched between the mountains and Sitkalidak Strait, we sat down to meals that would have made the finest chefs turn green with envy.

We had three or four tree plantings in Old Harbor, in which the women and children of the village all participated. Very few men and older boys were there because of fishing season. The entire year's income is earned in those few weeks each year when the men go to sea after salmon, bottom fish, and crab.

We planted several hundred trees in three or four locations, some of which were open to the weather, while some were protected by buildings or bushes. There was fairly good soil at some of the sites, and in others, little but the gravel left behind by the last of the glaciers. At last report, the Sitka spruce we planted were doing well, as we expected. A couple of the deciduous species have also fared well, while others have not.

In 1991, the year ReTree did a big project in Iceland, we sent my son, John, who is studying forest ecology, to Alaska. We had tree plantings scheduled at Kotzebue, Nome, St. Michael, Bethel, St. Mary's, and other targets of opportunity as they presented themselves. I wanted to go, but my associates in ReTree insisted that I had to show up in Iceland.

Chapter 12

John Lockyear:

I flew from Portland to Kotzebue, a village at the entrance of Kotzebue Sound on the eastern shore of the Chukchi Sea, north of Norton Sound. Kotzebue is above the Arctic Circle, so in mid-summer the sun doesn't set. It just circles the horizon twenty-four hours a day. I suppose after a person becomes acclimated, he can sleep well enough. But despite the fact that I hit town after thirty-six hours of no sleep, I was wide-eyed. Zombie-like, but awake.

Immediately after landing, I was dragooned into the high school gymnasium where the Inupiat people were having a dance. We Caucasians tend to lump all native peoples into one big group—we talk about American Indians, yet these people consider themselves Cree, Blackfeet, Hopi, and so forth. The people we call Eskimos also prefer to be known by their group names. The Inupiat are people who live in northern Alaska along the coastline. Certain Eskimos in Canada call themselves Inuit. In eastern Siberia, one of the groups is called the Yup'ik.

I'll never forget the dance the Inupiats held in the school gym. I got involved because the contact my father had chosen to coordinate things up there was interested in social activities in the village. I was just part of the audience of course, and it was only by chance that my arrival coincided with the event. It was a story-telling dance, accompanied by pan drums. The dancers were dressed in Eskimo garb—parkas and so forth, but because it was high summer, these were made of light-weight cotton. The storyline of the dance was about a young man who had to hunt to feed his people. He became lost and had to eat his dog to stay alive. In so doing, he absorbed the dog's spirit and when he returned to the people with food, all he could say was "woof, woof, woof."

The local coordinator had arranged for each Kotzebue family he knew to get two or three little trees, and that was largely what we did. But he didn't have a count of the seedlings needed, so we had a surplus. A lot of people who participated in the group tree planting were those I gave seedlings to. I asked them to come out to a tree planting at the Senior Center, and I got on the bush radio to announce the event.

Most of the Arctic, especially north of the Brooks Range, is treeless. Just tundra and muskeg. But around Kotzebue there is a healthy stand of balsam poplar growing right in the village. My guess is that it's been there since the end of the Pleistocene. Some of the trees are quite tall. They grow to the tops of the buildings, then are sheared off by the wind, and don't get any taller. There are several species of willows in the Kotzebue region, some of them quite large. And Sitka alder grows there. No conifers, but the archeological evidence indicates that they were in the area after the last Ice Age. My guess is that the first people who migrated from Asia consumed them.

There is pretty good soil in the region. Some of it is organic; most consists of fine mineral loess, a fine, wind-deposited loam. The Kotzebue region was not glaciated during the Ice Age. It was part of Berengia, which was probably covered with tundra, hardly a lush place, but attractive enough to lure game animals and the hunters who followed them.

I was assigned to work with a representative of the U.S. Forest Service, a lady who came out from Pennsylvania. She had trouble adjusting to the rather primitive conditions and left after a couple of days.

I think it probably takes a certain type of person to feel comfortable with the kind of work ReTree does. You have to have a feeling for what the organization is trying to do, some sense of commitment to trees, their importance to the world, and the need to plant them. I think some people think of tree planting as just something Boy Scouts and schoolchildren do. But my father is involved in the planting of *forest* trees. He wants to see idle lands around the world growing trees that once grew there, or that are ecologically compatible. He doesn't want to plant just one tree in a schoolyard. He wants each of his projects to end up with hundreds or thousands of trees in the ground. So the people who work with him have to be willing to get their hands and clothing dirty. They have to be willing to plant trees in blizzards and rainstorms, on steep hillsides and in the bottoms of canyons. They have to be willing to sack out in sleeping bags thrown on somebody's floor, or in an abandoned military barracks someplace. ReTree volunteers have to be willing to put in long, long hours on airplanes, shuttling across time zones, losing sleep, eating strange and sometimes unpalatable food. And when they reach their destination, they have to be enthusiastic and ready to go, to lead the people who are waiting to help. Planting trees my father's way isn't a romantic thing. It's hard, grueling work. And the people who do it best are those who have gone beyond the romance of saving the planet and are willing to be grunts. Some people can do this. Others can't.

Of course, there are rewards. There have to be for anybody to put up with all this. There is the knowledge that you *are* doing something for our planet, that planting trees is a very important thing to do. And there are the people. The local people we meet and work with are absolutely wonderful. We travel out to some village way out in the bush, and there are people eager to plant trees. Maybe they have never thought about a tree before in their lives. But they are there with shovels and enthusiasm. We meet some truly wonderful people.

Nina Lie is an Inupiat woman who has lived in Kotzebue all her life. When she was younger, she was connected with the jade-mining industry. The area is famous for its nephritic jade.

Nina worked for the post office in Kotzebue most of

her working life and when she retired, they awarded her P.O. Box #1, somewhat like an NFL team retiring a player's number. Nina lives in a nice little cottage in the village. These days, in her eighties, she still does beautiful skin sewing in the traditional manner. And she gardens! There in the Arctic she grows flowers and a fantastic vegetable garden. She has apple and citrus trees planted in tubs mounted on rollers. In the summer they are rolled outside to soak up sunlight twenty-four hours a day. In winter they are rolled back inside, out of fifty- and sixty-below-zero temperatures. Nina is very knowledgeable about and interested in the environment, and she wanted three spruce trees to plant near her cottage. I was delighted to give them to her and to suggest how best to make them live. It's a procedure we use in the Aleutians, where the wind can almost tear the little seedlings out of the ground. We plant them in five-gallon buckets that have the bottoms punched out. We water them thoroughly until they get established, then maybe prune them for the first year or two. If any spruce trees made it at Kotzebue, my guess is that they would be the ones Nina Lie planted near her little cottage.

From Kotzebue I flew across the Seward Peninsula to Nome. A beautiful flight. It was an unusually clear day in that part of the world and I could see right out to the horizon. Pack ice floated in the sea, and off to the west, I could see the Chukchi Peninsula in Siberia. I saw the Diomedes Islands and King and St. Lawrence Islands. Working as a ReTree volunteer has its perks.

Two of the Diomedes are just a few miles apart. The smaller is U.S. territory, the larger is Russian. Just sixty miles of open water—the Bering Strait—separates the two countries. Back in the Ice Ages, all of this was part of Berengia.

We got to Nome on the wrong day. Arrangements had been made at Wilsonville for us to be there three days later, so we didn't have a place to stay. But we were able to contact the president of the Lions Club, a man who had lived in Wilsonville, Oregon, before coming to Alaska.

He knew my father, and I guess he still had some pretty strong feelings left over from his Oregon days. He wore a T-shirt with a message that suggested he liked to eat spotted owl roasted! He invited us into his own home, cooked for us, and put us up for the night. He had an extra bed for the Forest Service lady, who left the expedition while we were at Nome. I slept out on the deck, which was high enough above the water to keep the mosquitoes away. Our host did a lot of telephoning and arranged for the native corporation to get us a hotel room.

The native corporation in Nome is called Sitnasuak. The closest I can come to the correct pronunciation is Sit-n-a-sack. It seems to be doing pretty well financially, unlike some of the other corporations. The gold fields at Nome have not run out, and are probably as rich as ever. There is as much gold being taken out as during the gold rush days at the turn of the century. The native corporation goes around buying defunct mining claims, mostly small ones, then rehabilitating them. They're doing quite well in this business. The winter after I was up there, they sent me a Christmas card, gold-plated.

We had plantings for two days in Nome, planting with native people and Girl Scouts. They went very well.

Nome is on a south-facing slope near the west end of the Seward Peninsula. There are hills to the north, but it's obvious that whatever timber was there has been consumed. Now the trees consist of Sitka alder and willow, which is probably good because they are a basis for a boreal forest ecosystem. Alder has nodules which fix the nitrogen into a usable form. Willow catches the organic debris that floats around and helps build humus.

The tundra grows back slowly after it has been disrupted by mining. My guess is that in about four hundred to five hundred years it will all be back. Right now there is a lot of muskeg—sphagnum moss interlaced with various low-lying willows and other shrubs. Usually it is very wet and difficult to plant trees in because the mineral soil, best for tree planting, can be far below the surface. There is apt to be permafrost under the muskeg, sometimes fairly deep, other times close to the surface. It's murder to plant trees where there is permafrost near the surface. The hole freezes back in the winter and pushes the tree right out. These frost heaves let the tree dry out and die.

A couple of days after the two tree plantings at Nome, I was supposed to go to the village of St. Michael. I took my stuff to the airport, then—because there was plenty of time until the flight—went to a cafe for coffee. I met a fascinating person there, a man named Hunter Michaelbrink. He is a teacher of agriculture at the local community college, although, from my observations, there isn't much by way of agriculture in the area.

Hunter has contacts with some groups of Siberian Yup'iks who moved onto the Seward Peninsula from Siberia. These are Eskimos who left the Chukchi Peninsula because as migratory people they were having a hard time under the Soviets. When the Communist regime started to fall apart, they asked permission to leave, and came across from Siberia in skin umiaks and aluminum boats. There are probably three or four groups of two hundred living on the peninsula now. Other Yup'iks living in the Yukon Delta have been there since the Russians came to Alaska in the eighteenth century.

The Yup'iks on the Seward Peninsula live near the water in huts and shacks, and range inland to hunt. Living conditions are tough. They harvest from the land—berries and roots—all good-quality food but sometimes scarce. They fish and take bowhead whales, one of which can feed a lot of people for a long time. I met some of the Yup'iks, and although they didn't speak English very well we had little trouble communicating. Those who have come in the last few years pretty much stay to themselves. They're far enough out that they don't eat at McDonalds or drive snowmobiles, but they are into tennis shoes and polyester clothing. And Coca Cola.

After dropping off my stuff at the airport, I took a look around town. As I walked on the beach, I ran into a medical student who comes up from Pennsylvania each year when school ends. He flies to Alaska and starts panning the beach, where he works until school starts in the fall. His take, by working all the waking hours of the day and not leaving the beach, is running about fifty-four thousand dollars a year. He told me that that day he had already panned about an ounce and a half of gold— roughly six hundred dollars' worth.

I talked with another young man on the beach who wasn't working as hard as the medical student. He'd pan just a little bit of gold each day, then put it into little glass vials. He'd add a bit of sea water, seal the vials, then sell them to tourists for thirty dollars each. He was mining the tourists.

People in Nome can't stake a legal claim on the beach; it's open territory. Anybody can walk out on the beach and start panning. Your territory is as much as your personality—and a stainless steel pistol—can control. A person works the area where he is; nobody crowds his neighbor. I saw a lot of people in their little areas, panning or working little power sluices in areas about thirty feet in diameter. If a guy went into town to have supper, nobody moved in to high-grade him. I did see a couple of people who had pistols lying out in the open where anybody could see them, so they backed up neighborliness with firepower.

There is still gold on the Nome beaches because of the sea. It keeps churning the bottom, exposing more of the gold-bearing sand, which is a pretty magenta color. Garnet sand. The gold lies in a subsurface layer that goes back to the base of the hills.

I wandered back out to the airport to wait for my flight, which was still several hours away. As I was sitting there, a young fellow came up and said, "Hey, do you want to go to Russia?"

I said, "Of course. But I don't have papers. No visa or anything. What's the deal?"

"You can go along as a cargo handler. You'll have to stay with the airplane. You can't wander around. Want to go?"

We flew across the Bering Strait to Provodenya in Siberia, then onto Anadyr. I could look down onto Russian soil and see the lay of the land on the Chukchi Peninsula. It's a lot like western Alaska. The main difference is that I didn't see places where people have dug ditches with bulldozers. And I didn't see any "Alaska gardens"—junk piles of sheet metal, empty fifty-gallon drums, abandoned machinery. Instead of roads where people force their way through with three-wheelers in the winter, I saw game trails.

We flew from Anadyr to Magadan, a city of about half a million people, established by the Soviets during WWII as a place to relocate factories away from the Germans. If you draw a great circle from Portland, Oregon, through Anchorage, through Nome, you get to Magadan. In Magadan, some Russians came out to the airplane. One of them, a medical doctor, knew a little English, and I knew a little Russian. He gave me a map of the area and an anniversary pin that celebrated the founding of the city half a century earlier. After Magadan, we turned around and flew back to Nome, all in one day.

The next day I flew around the end of Norton Sound, to the village of St. Michael. At the turn of the century, this was an important place in the Klondike Gold Rush. It was the port where the first of those who struck it rich on the Klondike River emerged from the interior. They struggled aboard the two steamships anchored at St. Michael, the *Portland* and the *Excelsior*, toting suitcases, leather and canvas bags, trunks, even bedrolls, filled with gold. When they reached the lower forty-eight, and as news of their find reached the world, St. Michael became the port of entry to Alaska for gold seekers who came north by sea. That's where they transferred from oceangoing ships to stern-wheelers for the long trip up the Yukon. In those days, St. Michael was a tiny, wretched port on the Bering Sea, a place of drab mudflats, dismal, gray warehouses, and one rusting old Russian cannon. According to the journals, it stank of rotting fish. But it was the gateway to the Yukon, so people came by the thousands. And because of its location near the mouth of the Yukon River, it was a center for the shipment of much of the gold taken from the Klondike. When gold was discovered on the beaches at Nome, St. Michael became its port of departure to the outside world.

When I got out of the airplane at the St. Michael airport, the temperature was about forty-five degrees, the wind was blowing, and there wasn't a soul around. The plane took off and there I was. Eventually a three-wheeler showed up, driven by a Yup'ik who called himself Snowball. We put my gear on the back and we drove to the village about half a mile away. I wasn't expected. They didn't even know I was coming, because ReTree coordination in Wilsonville had confused St. Michael with St. Mary's, another village.

I made contact with the retired mayor and with the Roman Catholic priest and learned that most of the village people were away fighting forest fires. The priest thought we could get together some children from the school, and they turned out to be some of the nicest children I have ever had on any tree planting. They were also some of the most destitute. St. Michael is said to be the poorest place in North America. I especially remember two youngsters, Marjean Ooten and her brother Freddy. Marjean wore a paisley-cotton, pullover, Eskimo parka dress with the sleeves torn off it. That was the only clothing she owned. Freddy had a T-shirt, a sateen polyester jacket, a misfitting pair of blue jeans, and rubber boots. Those two kids kind of adopted me and followed me wherever I went. All the children in the village showed up to plant trees. Teenagers and everybody.

I've often been accused of carrying too much luggage with me. When I go someplace like Alaska, I take along a month's supply of dry food, and this time it really paid off. Not only did I eat my own food, but I was able to fix little treats for the kids who helped me. I fed them all the time I was there.

I was at St. Michael for three days, and stayed in the combination city hall and administrative center where there was hot water and a couch I could sleep on. With no place in town to buy food, I was really on my own.

When St. Michael was in its heyday, many people came from the outside, and many of them died there, so the area is dotted with cemeteries. After a tree planting at the Russian Orthodox graveyard, I planted trees in little groves in other cemeteries, and got to see ruins left from the old days.

Almost all of the wood used to build the town at the turn of the century has now been used as firewood. There are only fragments left of what was a large settlement. All that's left of the Russian Orthodox church is its onion dome, which sits on the ground minus its cross, which has been knocked off. The dome is constructed of perfectly fitted pieces of spruce painted with red lead and covered with galvanized sheet metal that is attached with square nails. It's about four feet tall and the same in diameter. The dome is tough enough to have withstood the climate and to have discouraged wood choppers. There it sits, all alone in the middle of the tundra.

From St. Michael I flew back to Nome, and headed for Bethel, a town of four or five thousand people on the Kuskokwim River on the south side of the Yukon Delta. Both the Yukon and Kuskokwim empty into the Bering Sea from this delta. At Bethel, I called a Yup'ik lady I know named Alice Criswell, who picked me up and took me to the home of Tim Meyers and his family. There a bunch of kids was ready to go tree planting, since I was supposed to have been there the previous day. I was tired, and the trees hadn't arrived, so I sent everyone home. Tim Meyers had some rooms for people to stay in, so I got one, got cleaned up, did some laundry, and got a good night's sleep. The next day I got together with representatives of the Boy and Girl Scouts, the 4-H, some churches, including the Moravian church, and we did tree plantings at the community college, and on church and cemetery properties all around town. During that day, we got about eight hundred trees planted, and had a lot of fun. About half the children were Eskimos. That evening I went to Alice Criswell's house for a salmon dinner that would have cost an arm and a leg outside.

The next day I flew out to the village of Kasigluk. I had been there planting trees a year or two before and wanted to see how the trees were doing. Unfortunately, they were all dead because of human, dog, and snowmobile traffic. Since the village hadn't expected me because of another scheduling snafu, a big festival was being held to raise money for the local Orthodox church, I couldn't get anybody to help plant trees. So I took off on my own to a grove of Sitka alder about a half mile outside of town. The alder would shield the conifer seedlings from the weather and help fix the nitrogen that they need. The next day I flew back to Bethel with a Yup'ik pilot.

Alice Criswell keeps me informed about the trees we planted around Bethel. There is a forty to fifty percent survival rate. Those we planted at the Meyers' residence are four and five feet tall. Tim Meyer had scavenged some trees that had survived an experimental nursery planted earlier by Dr. Alden, and he replanted them in sheltered areas, up on mounds to prevent frost heaving, and has kept them watered. Those trees have taken off like gangbusters.

Next I flew to St. Mary's, a village on the Yukon about one hundred miles north of Bethel. St. Mary's had been a fueling port for the stern-wheelers when they were on the Yukon. I'm told that some of those boats would burn a cord of wood an hour, especially when they were headed upstream, so it took a lot of trees to keep the vessels underway, and the forests along the river show it. They are all second growth, since everything was cut. The remains of woodcutter cabins exist on the Yukon from the delta upstream to Whitehorse in the Yukon Territory, the head of navigation on the river.

One of my friends was in Whitehorse in the winter of 1947. A narrow-gauge railroad, the White Pass and Yukon, goes through town, and he went down to the station to get tickets out to Skagway. There, chalked on the schedule board, was a notice. "First stern-wheeler: May 8, 1948."

Stern-wheelers were on the river until 1955, when air and highway traffic put them out of business.

While I was there, a group of Canadian Girl Scout leaders was visiting St. Mary's, teaching the native children how to swim. We had a couple of tree plantings with these young ladies and the local children. I stayed in the town for two nights and planted all the trees I had left. Had a real nice time with those people.

From St. Mary's I flew to Bethel, to Anchorage, and out to Portland, where my father and Allan de Lay met me. They were on their way to a tree planting at the Warm Springs Indian Reservation, and wanted me to go along. I was tired and wanted a warm bath and clean sheets, so I backed out. I had traveled just about all of the western end of Alaska, excluding the Aleutians. I had stayed in places that ranged in size from a town of several thousand people to tiny villages hugging the coastline. I had slept between clean, crisp sheets, and in my bag tossed on a deck overlooking the Bering Sea. I had eaten in restaurants that ranged from good to tolerable, and I had eaten the desiccated provisions I had hauled all the way from Oregon. I had flown to Russia, and hiked the tundra of my own nation. I had worked with some of the nicest, friendliest kids I have ever known, and together we had planted hundreds of trees.

Not too bad for just two weeks.

Chapter 13

Humans have cut down trees since before recorded time. They have cut them for fuel, shelter, war, commerce, and simply to get rid of them to make room for farms and cities. Europe and much of Asia lost their forests long ago, and the forests of the tropics are going today. In North America, the commercial cutting of trees reached its most organized state and almost cleared an entire continent of virgin forests.

When Europeans first came to the new world, they stepped onto a continent carpeted with three million square miles of forests. Forests stretched from the St. Lawrence River south to the Gulf of Mexico, and westward from the Atlantic to the Mississippi. They included some of the finest hardwood species in the world, and in the more northern latitudes, forests of magnificent conifers, including white pine. Over the hundreds of centuries these forests had been growing, they were untouched by humans. The few people who lived among them did little to disturb them.

The European settlers turned on the forests with axe and saw. To them, the forests were impediments. They held dangerous animals and, from the settlers' perspective, even more dangerous humans. Here, they thought, was an endless supply of trees, and they set out to exploit it.

The first sawmill on the continent was built in Maine in 1631. One of the earliest mill operators was John Alden, son of the man who proposed to Priscilla Mullins on behalf of Miles Standish, and ended up marrying her himself. In thirty years, more than five hundred vessels came off the ways of just one shipyard in New England.

Huge amounts of timber were shipped off to Europe, much of it destined for the English navy. In just three years in the mid-eighteenth century, New England loggers felled more than 240,000 trees as fuel for the Caribbean sugar mills.

The newly discovered continent acted as a people magnet. Millions of immigrants arrived and they needed food, homes, and employment. The forests were a major resource to draw on. Because New England's forests were so profuse, they were among the first to feel the axe. "Letting daylight into the swamp," it was called. Prime white pine was the main target species. Cedar was used for shingles if they were growing among the pine, and hemlock for its bark to sell to tanners. But the magnificent white pine of those northern woods was what the loggers and their bosses wanted.

Chapter 14

We did the project at Dutch Harbor in cooperation with the Ounalashka Corporation and its members, including President Kathy Grimnes and Vice President Barbara Rankin. The corporation is one of several native-owned corporations established by the Alaska Native Claims Act of 1971, by which lands that native peoples had lived on and used were apportioned to them. In cases where the economic value was very small, other public lands of greater worth and or potential were included in the holdings.

Without exception, ReTree enjoys excellent relations with the people of these corporations. They welcome our planting representatives, put them up, feed them, and supply vehicles for transportation, as well as volunteers to plant the trees. In the lower forty-eight, we have comparable cooperation with the Indian agencies we work with, and we conduct many projects each year on reservations throughout the West. In 1992 ReTree planted trees with twenty tribes.

The Warm Springs Reservation is across the Cascades from my home in Oregon. In the spring of 1992, I contacted foresters with the Bureau of Indian Affairs, inviting them to be partners with ReTree in a tree planting at Warm Springs. As is usually the case, the level of cooperation was great. The forester found a site on the reservation that would be safe from livestock; he furnished the seedlings; and he found a couple of adult volunteers who were willing to work alongside me with the children. I contacted an old Scouting friend, Ray Peyralans, from Troop 66, to go over to central Oregon with me. He said he'd be delighted and offered the use of his pickup. I met him one beautiful spring morning, and we set off.

On the way over the mountain, we stopped at a small restaurant alongside the highway for breakfast. Having plenty of time, we chatted leisurely about this and that, looking forward to a pleasant day. But when we went out to get going, Ray's pickup wouldn't start. We tried and tried. No go. We pushed it out onto the road and headed downhill to jump-start it. Still no go. We coasted down a couple of miles to the tiny town of Zig Zag, named for the river that flows nearby, which, during the winter of 1964 when there was a sudden melt of the snow pack, zigzagged down the main street. We pulled into a service station, went inside, and looked for the owner, but there didn't seem to be anyone around.

"Anybody here?"

"I'm here."

We spotted a lady lying back there with a blanket over her. She pushed it aside and came out to the counter, saying "I catch a nap when things are slow."

I had been in the station a few weeks earlier with my friend Allan de Lay on our way to another tree planting, and the lady remembered me. After we explained our problem, she suggested we call a tow truck. We were still okay on time, and Warm Springs was just a half-hour away, so we didn't feel pressured. But when the tow truck driver took a look at the pickup, he shook his head and suggested we get towed still farther back down the highway to his station for safekeeping. Now I began to get just a little bit nervous. I asked the lady who had been napping for some suggestions about how we might get to Warm Springs.

"Give me a few minutes," she said. She dropped the blanket, put a shawl over her shoulders, and left the station. Time ticked away. Eventually, she came back and announced that she had somebody who would take us over the mountain.

"They have a van. It stinks something terrible. But the boys are willing to take you to Warm Springs," she said.

That sounded pretty good.

"They don't have any gas, though."

I gave her a fifty-dollar bill and she disappeared. In a few minutes she was back with the boys and their van. It was kind of rundown. It was terribly rundown. I wondered if we'd see Warm Springs. The lady put twenty dollars worth of gas in the tank, and gave me the change, which I turned over to the three boys. We climbed into the van and drove away.

The boys didn't speak English very well, and I wondered how long they had been north of the border. They were nice kids, though, and seemed to look forward to seeing the Indian reservation. I had my doubts if any of us would see it the way they were driving. There was no speedometer, so I couldn't tell exactly how fast we were going, but it was enough to throw me from side to side when we went around turns. The seat I was on wasn't fastened to the van, and had a mind of its own on the turns.

When we reached the reservation, a school bus filled with children was waiting for us. I had called ahead, explaining why we might be late. The children were young, maybe third or fourth graders, and the teacher had her hands full trying to keep them settled down. I invited the three boys in the van to join us, but they figured that they'd just wait for us there. That seemed all right. Besides, what could I do, drag them along? Maybe I should have.

Well, the tree planting went well. The forester I had talked with earlier was there with a pickup of trees, a few shovels, and some water he had hauled in to give the seedlings a good drink when they were in the ground. At the planting site, he instructed the children about how to plant trees. There were about twenty-five children, and they planted about one hundred trees. Ray Peyralans and I worked beside them.

Ray is a very good tree planter. Why wouldn't he be? I taught him how to move trees more than fifty years ago.

After the trees were in the ground and the children had had refreshments, we climbed onto the bus and drove forty miles back to where we had left the three boys and their van. They weren't there. The situation seemed to be getting a bit out of hand. Eventually, they showed up. Was it my imagination, or was the van weaving a bit as it came down the road?

As we climbed in and took off up the highway toward Zig Zag, I noticed the boys had a case of beer. What ensued was a very exciting ride. I can't say how fast we were going, but I'll bet it was somewhere between ninety and one hundred. My guess is that they had spent the money I had given them on beer, and that the case in the van was just the last survivor.

Ray is a Catholic, and whenever I looked over at him I could see his lips moving as he prayed.

When we climbed out of the van at Zig Zag, I handed the driver a ten-dollar tip. I figure that I lost more than one hundred dollars in those few hours, and Ray had to have his pickup towed more than forty miles back to a garage in Portland, where he was charged another four hundred dollars for repairs.

We have conducted tree plantings on reservations from Montana to New Mexico, and each one has been a delightful experience. The children are so eager and excited about planting their very own trees. For many of these youngsters, it is the first time they will have been out in nature. This seems strange, until you understand the circumstances. It is true that most of the reservations are well away from cities, so a person would expect that the children would have an entire world of nature to play in and explore. But the sad fact is that most of them are desperately poor. Life isn't a romp in wildflowers and among trees; it is a struggle for survival. And when you are hungry, you don't have much interest in exploring nature or anything else. It is mainly through the schools that these children are introduced to a larger world than the sad, impoverished one they know so well. But I think that children are basically pretty much the same worldwide, and given the chance, will respond to a positive experience like planting a tree. This is especially true when they have some idea of why they are planting it, so before the actual event, we emphasize what will happen.

When a tree planting is finally scheduled, we recommend that the children receive an indoctrination in the classroom before going out to the site. By "indoctrination," I mean study units on what trees are, what forests are, what trees and forests contribute to the planet's well-being, and what they mean to our economy and recreation. We suggest that a brief history of human relations with trees be covered to give the children a smattering of information about what has happened, and is happening, to the world's forests. All of this shouldn't be dragged on and on. But a good study unit, well-presented, can go a long way to make the actual planting of trees more meaningful.

It's also important that there be a follow-up to the event. What did we do? Where did we do it? What kind of country was it? What was the weather? What kinds of trees did we plant? How many?

At one very successful project with a school group in Montana, it was obvious that a great amount of preparation had been done by the school. The children knew why they were out there planting trees, what they were planting, and something about how to plant. Their teachers were there, kneeling in the soil and getting dirty along with them. They told me that some of the pictures taken that day would be published in the school's yearbook, and that the following year, these same children would take another field trip to the planting site to check up on the trees. It's my bet that at least some of these children will stay involved in trees and forests into their adult lives.

We have planted with children from the Apache, Zuni, and Jicarilla tribes as well as the Rosebud and Oglala Sioux.

Before our first trip to the Southwest, I assumed we'd be working in river bottoms or other moist areas in a land that was otherwise all desert. But in each case, the planting site was one in which trees not only *could* grow, but were already growing.

For example, one of our projects with the Apaches involved driving into the White Mountains six thousand feet above sea level. There was the prettiest ponderosa pine forest I have ever seen. These trees are on the Fort Apache Reservation, and are thus the property of the tribe, where people log and run cattle up there. They have a professional forester who advises them in the management of their forest, and the quality of the logging shows the effect of this. It is ecologically sound.

I was much impressed with what I saw.

A few years ago, we drove to Grants, New Mexico, on Interstate 40, about eighty miles west of Albuquerque. Grants had seen far better days back in the 1950s, when the uranium deposits in the area caused the place to boom. Now it has slipped back into being a small agricultural town sandwiched in a valley between the north and south units of the Cibola National Forest. We drove up into the south units in company with rangers from the forest on the morning of the tree planting. We were going to plant trees in cooperation with the Izaac Walton League riparian enhancement effort, led by one of ReTree's best friends, Patricia Honeycut. While she and her crew were planting willows along the streams, we planted ponderosa pine on the bench lands. The planting went well and the high school children who participated did a good job.

But the planting site was not fenced—there were plenty of meadow muffins lying around. In fact, we broke some of them up to fertilize the little seedlings. I haven't checked on those seedlings we planted, but I'm afraid they didn't survive. Cattle, otherwise known as horned locusts, probably made short work of them.

We had some time to kill before the planting, so we went sightseeing. The Native Americans in the Grants, New Mexico, area are Pueblo people. Acoma is one of the oldest, continuously occupied pueblos in the country. Established in 1250 A.D., or earlier, it is on a 357-foot-high sandstone mesa overlooking the San Jose River Valley. The name comes from the native word, Akóne. At one time more than fifteen hundred people lived in the village. Only a handful remain. The rest of the people live in villages in the river valley. The church, San Esteban Rey, built or rebuilt after a fire in 1699, is a beautiful example of the adobe architecture of the times. Its walls are more than two feet thick; its roof is supported by massive log beams, probably of ponderosa pine, taken from the nearby mountains. There is no floor, just dirt. I had hoped to see the interiors of the houses, but although visitors are welcome in the village, they are not allowed to wander freely. They travel in groups led by native guides.

It was in such old ruins, even older than those at Acoma, that discoveries were made that led to a new science based on the tree's growth rings. By counting the rings, we determine the tree's age. And by studying their width, we get a pretty good picture of short-term and long-term climate. Wide rings mean plenty of moisture, narrow rings, drought.

Dr. A. E. Douglass of the University of Arizona applied this tree-ring information to studies of longer-term changes in climate. The result is the discipline called dendrochronology, the science of tree time.

A dendrochronologist compares the earliest rings of a living tree with the last rings laid down in a piece of dead wood from the same species and the same site. If the dates of the two wood samples overlap, the spacings of early rings from the living wood will match the latest rings from the dead. So long as increasingly older wood samples are available, the scientist can work back in time almost indefinitely in a process called cross dating.

Dr. Douglass was dating pueblo ruins in Arizona by studying the annular rings in wood beams used in their construction when he realized he had stepped into a time warp that took him back beyond known historical time.

He expanded his studies and developed the broad uses to which dendrochronology is now put. In addition to time, he measured ancient environmental conditions. What had been the rainfall a thousand years or so ago? What were the soil conditions? What kinds of winds were blowing? Dendrochronology gives the scientist a window into the past from which inferences can be drawn about the future.

I was quite serious when I told a group of Zuni children that we EuroAmericans have a debt to pay for what our forefathers did to their lands. We do have such an obligation and I feel privileged to do my part to help pay it. We owe it not only to these people, but to the Earth itself. The Native Americans realize that the Earth is our Great Mother, that we are all beholden to her, and we destroy her lands and forests at our own peril. So the tree planting we in ReTree do is undertaken with a real appreciation of its seriousness.

Nonetheless, tree planting can be fun. It should be fun, especially for the children. I remember a planting we did with the Zunis in New Mexico. After the event, the high school kids assembled in a group for a picture. Allan de Lay was going to get some video footage for the record. He got them all together, then said, "Now everybody say 'Cheese!'" That reminded me of an incident that happened when we did a Mexico planting, and I told the Zuni kids about it.

"We were down in Mexico planting with some gung-ho boys, about your age. They were real strong. They had been working out. That day they got up at six in the morning so they could work out a couple of hours before we went tree planting. After we finished, they were up in the truck and I wanted to get them to smile for a picture, so I said, 'Now say *cheese!*' Well, those boys threw up their hands and jumped up and down, howling with laughter. They slapped each other and pointed at me, and laughed even more. Their teacher came up to me and said, 'Frank, the next time you address my students, don't say "cheese." If you want them to smile, maybe you should whistle or do something silly. In Spanish, cheese means to go to the bathroom.'"

When we were in New Mexico, one of the planting sites was a ponderosa pine forest that had been burned.

The tribal forester, Roger Jenson, explained this to the children.

"As you can see by looking around, we had a disastrous fire in this area about four years ago, caused by high school students who were partying. We wish very much they had not left their campfire burning. Because of their activity, we lost nearly all the understory of ponderosa pine in this area."

The fire hadn't covered a very large area, and the mature trees appeared to me to have survived, even though they were scorched. Maybe all the seedlings we planted that day will help restore the understory and become part of the mature forest when they grow.

During the 1980s, ReTree worked with handicapped children at the Kiwanis' Mt. Hood Camp for the Handicapped. This summer camp, which has been in operation since 1933, is located in the Douglas fir forests on the western slopes of Mt. Hood. Each year it offers an eight-week program for 320 youngsters aged nine through twenty-one. The children can participate in the usual summer camp activities—fishing, horseback riding, hiking, overnight outings, campfires, and so forth. I thought there might be still another activity they might enjoy, so in 1984, in cooperation with the camp, we began tree plantings. These were some of our earliest experiments in working with handicapped children, and without exception, they were a success. About 1990 when the camp was being enlarged, the disruptions associated with construction caused us to temporarily discontinue the tree plantings. But I was encouraged by the response and involvement of these handicapped children, and hoped to continue working with them in other areas. I got in touch with officials at the Washington State School for the Blind, and proposed that we conduct a special tree planting for their students. The response was very enthusiastic. The next challenge was to find a site. The school didn't have one, and I wasn't comfortable transporting the children out to Forest Service land in the mountains.

I remembered that back in my Lambert Gardens days, Mr. Lambert had leased land from Reed College to use as a nursery for some of his plants. I didn't know what happened to that land after Mr. Lambert closed his company, but it was easy to find out. I turned to the tool I use the most in the tree-planting business. I picked up the phone.

A few years ago, a person who wrote a magazine article about my activities said that I make telephone calls around the world as casually as most people call their neighbors. I guess he was right.

The key to a successful tree planting is the planning, which takes time and many, many contacts with whatever groups are involved. I suppose I could handle the arrangements by mail, but this would involve even more time, and would not be as efficient as talking directly with the people involved. So I use the phone. The person who wrote that magazine article added that my phone bill approximates the national debt.

When I called Reed College, I learned that the school still had plenty of land on which to plant trees. And when I explained our needs for the project involving disabled school children, it was made available. One of the advantages of the site is that buses can be driven very close to it, and this was an important consideration for the children.

The initial tree planting was so successful that we expanded the idea to include deaf and retarded children. Of course, because each group has its own special considerations, we conduct the plantings separately.

These outings are great opportunities for the children. We try to make a special effort to tell them what an important contribution they are making just by getting on their hands and knees and working with the earth.

I especially remember one lady with whom I planted a tree. She was probably in her thirties, and had the mental ability of a young child. The delight on her face when she realized that she was planting something that would grow in the soil was a joy to see.

Chapter 15

An exotic plant or animal is one that has been introduced into an environment from a foreign country. I avoid taking exotic species to an area, unless the tree planting is a scientific experiment, like the one at Old Harbor, or a special case, like the planting of firs at the David Douglas monument, or when a certain species has been proven to be the only one or one of very few that can fill certain needs.

There are ethical reasons for my reluctance to introduce exotica. In the first place, our main goal is to help reforest places we visit. And the *re* part of the equation means reintroducing species that were there before, not introducing new ones. Even in the case of afforestation—which is planting trees where they haven't existed before—we pick species that would logically be found there.

We work closely with foresters and forest scientists in choosing species. Early in the organizing of a tree-planting project, I contact state or federal foresters in the area to get their recommendations regarding the species to be planted. Of course, I also try to enlist their help.

There are many examples of what can happen when exotica are introduced. In my area of the Pacific Northwest, for example, we are plagued with a bush called Scotch broom. This is a tough plant that produces yellow blossoms in late spring. As you might expect, it is a native of the British Isles. Somebody brought it to the Northwest many years ago, and it has gone crazy, taking over open fields, and destroying hay crops and pasturage.

Another example from my part of the country is the

Himalayan blackberry. This is not a native, yet is found in almost every sunny place west of the Cascade Mountains. It produces wonderful berries, and reproduces fantastically. So it's almost impossible to control except by using powerful herbicides. Even though they don't eliminate the plant, they do slow it down for a season or two.

The dandelion so hated by lawn lovers is also an import from England. So is the English, or house, sparrow. The bird, a native of Eurasia and North Africa, was introduced into the United States from England in 1851. It has replaced many native birds because of its pugnaciousness and adaptability. I've seen one English sparrow keep an entire flock of Oregon juncos, a small member of the finch family, completely away from a feeder. Then there is the starling. Native to Europe, Africa, Asia, and Australia, the bird was introduced to North America and Hawaii where it became a real nuisance, annoying local birds and often stealing their nesting sites. The starling truly deserves its scientific name, *Sturnus vulgaris*.

There are countless examples of the harm exotic animals can cause, and the Hawaiian Islands presents one of the more dramatic. They were "discovered" in 1778 by Captain James Cook, who named them the Sandwich Islands in honor of his patron, the Earl of Sandwich. Of course, the islands had been discovered centuries earlier by the ancestors of the people Cook found living there. They had come in canoes more than two thousand miles from Polynesia in about 750 A.D. They brought entire families, old cultures, and the hula. They also brought along exotica.

The only truly indigenous mammal in Hawaii is a small bat. The first Hawaiians brought dogs, pigs, mice, and rats, the first two deliberately, the others as stowaways. They also introduced coconuts, breadfruit, Malay apple, (also called ohia) taro, sweet potatoes, yams, bananas, and more than a dozen other plants, including sugar cane.

When the Europeans settled in Hawaii, they brought goats, cattle, sheep, horses, Axis deer, oranges and other citrus fruits, avocados, mangos, coffee, grapes, figs, and that nut that is considered the very essence of Hawaii, the macadamia.

Although there were rats in Hawaii before white men arrived, the explorers and whalers who made port in the islands brought them in profusion, especially the big Norwegian rat. This is the creature we think of when the very word "rat" is mentioned. Because there were no natural predators in Hawaii to control the rat population, it exploded. The rats attacked native birds, eating their eggs, chicks, and even adults. Many of the more than 125 species of native birds were brought to the edge of extinction. Some became extinct. In an effort to save the birds, the mongoose was introduced from Asia to kill the rats. This it did, with great gusto, but it also turned on the birds. With whatever rats were left, plus the pigs and hogs the whalers turned loose, the exotic carnivores just about finished off most of Hawaii's magnificent bird species.

A similar state of affairs occurred in Jamaica. Mongooses brought to Jamaica to control rats that were destroying sugar cane also killed off many native animal species.

David Douglas discovered an exotic plant during one of his field trips to central California—wild oats (*Avena fatua*). This was a common weed grass in Europe in Douglas' time and its seeds may have been transported to America by the Spanish in straw used for wrapping fragile items.

When Douglas discovered the patch of oats in 1831, it covered just a few acres. Four years later, it had spread northward on the peninsula that separates San Francisco Bay from the Pacific. By 1855, just twenty-four years after Douglas first saw it, wild oats covered the entire Coast Range and the Central Valley, a carpet, according to one observer, "as complete as buffalo grass on a prairie." Today, wild oats spreads throughout California from Redding to the Mexican border. And it is only one of the 526 alien plants that have been introduced into the state over the years. It is, in fact, the plant that gives the Golden State its name.

This might seem innocent enough, until one wonders what native grasses were pushed aside by the intruder. Recently, some innovative investigators took adobe bricks from buildings erected by the Spanish in early California. Adobe bricks, of course, are made of earth that is pressed into molds and sunbaked. Their importance to investigators lay in whatever seeds were in the earth used to make the adobe. The bricks were pounded to dust, analyzed, and found to contain large amounts of annual and perennial clover and bunch grass seeds. The clover had been especially important to the soil because of its nitrogen-fixing characteristics. Paradoxically, it helped exterminate the native grasses by providing rich natural fertilizer for the first few crops of wild oats.

Native species of animals and plants are where they are because they developed there, in partnership with other species, over thousands of years. They adapted to the conditions of the habitat—climate, food supply, soil, predators—and unless disturbed, continue to exist in the balance that nature demands of its life forms.

When a species is taken into another habitat, one of several things is apt to happen. The species might not be able to exist in the new environment, which might be too cold, too hot, too dry, or too damp, or otherwise unable to provide what the species needs. Or the new environment might be just barely good enough to allow the plant or animal to get along. The third possibility, and probably the worst one, is that the interloper finds itself in hog heaven, with plenty of whatever it needs to thrive. The predators it had to cope with back home aren't around, and those in place haven't figured out how to handle this intruder. The species then takes off and overwhelms the environment. It becomes a dominant life form, and an ecological disaster of sorts takes place.

San Clemente is one of the Channel Islands off the coast of southern California. A U.S. Navy facility uses a small part of the island for artillery practice. The island is, or was, home to thousands of feral goats, the parental stock of whom were dropped there early in the nineteenth century by whalers. The goats had served as a supply of fresh meat. Lacking any natural predators and able to eat just about anything, the goats thrived and overran the island, stripping it of its grass and leaving cactus in its stead. San Clemente was on the way to becoming a desert punctuated by shell holes.

When the Endangered Species Act became law, the Navy, like all other government agencies, was required to protect native species. On San Clemente, that meant taking care of the goats. Trapping was tried. The trapped goats were then offered for adoption, but for some reason, they died when on the mainland. Some were taken onto the firebreaks that scar the ridge lines in southern California's Coast Range. The goats were supposed to reduce the fire danger by eating the grass in the breaks. They did eat the grass there, and everywhere else; they wouldn't stay in the breaks. Finally, the Navy had to revert to the ultimate solution. Now, the native grasses and wildflowers have come back to San Clemente.

We humans do not have the right to wreak ecological havoc on our planet. If I present myself as a person whose goal is to plant trees on idle lands around the world, I have the responsibility to plant species that are already there, that were there before being wiped out, or, which are compatible with existing plants and animals.

Chapter 16

As service clubs go, the Lions are noted for their good deeds in the community, and Walter Trandum is a Lion. Walter, a retired phone company employee, wondered why so many phone books were being dumped in landfills. He got no reasonable answers, so he started a phone book recycling program, and while he was at it, one for newspapers too. This was many years before the current recycling program was even a glimmer in anyone's eye.

There are 41,500 Lions Clubs in 177 countries and geographic locations around the world. Total membership is almost 1.5 million. No matter where ReTree develops a tree-planting project, there is a Lions Club handy. We haven't called on all 41,500 yet, but we're working on it. Getting Lions' help usually involves little more than picking up the phone.

Lions are especially helpful in supplying refreshments at our tree plantings. It seems a small thing to give children a few cookies and a soda after they plant trees, but it's a nice way to say "Thank you for coming out to help our beautiful planet."

Recently we went to Puerto Rico on a project. One phone call to local Lions Clubs assured refreshments for the children.

There were many Boy Scouts and Girl Scouts at the event, plus children from early elementary grades. When I go on these tree plantings, I carry a small, blue duffle bag loaded with little pins in the shape of trees, which we give to the children. In Puerto Rico, I simply upended the bag and let the kids scramble for the goodies that fell out. Afterwards, one of the leaders came up to me and said her girls wanted to kiss me for giving them all those nice things. They all lined up and gave me a big kiss as they passed. I had to kneel to get down to their height. It was like being the guest of honor in a reception line.

Although Puerto Rico is a part of the United States, at least for the time being, it has a decidedly foreign flavor. The language, of course, is Spanish and the architecture, at least the old architecture, is colonial Spanish. The people from the Department of Natural Resources were kind enough to take me and my friend Hinkey Foleen around San Juan. The new parts of the city, with the fast food stores and glass and concrete factories, are changing the character of the place. But in the older parts of town, and certainly in the country, the scene is much as it probably was a few hundred years ago.

Soon after establishing ReTree, I began contacting various governments suggesting that we work together planting trees in their countries. This was in the time of the Iron Curtain and Cold War, so I was surprised when Poland expressed interest, but I wasn't about to let politics intrude into something critical for the whole world. My wife and I made the trip to Poland in 1979, courtesy of Pan American Airways, taking fourteen boxes of tree seedlings contributed by the Crown Zellerbach Corporation.

Jean and I arrived in Warsaw April 1, 1980, when the weather was too cold to unpack the trees outside. We had to unpack them in a greenhouse. Because Poland was still under a Communist government, they weren't supposed to have a Boy Scout organization, but they did. There was also an American Boy Scout troop in Warsaw, made up boys who went to the American school. Most of these children were not American nationals, but children of embassy personnel from various nations who were stationed in Warsaw. There were about twenty of them, and they all came to our tree planting at the Children's Hospital in Warsaw. The two Boy Scout groups, American and Polish, planted trees side-by-side. Afterwards, we had a little get-together, and I gave all the Polish Scouts a little tree and a City of Portland rose sticker. They all seemed appreciative.

Before we left Oregon, Dr. Sam Foster, a scientist with Crown Zellerbach, arranged with Polish officials for an experimental planting of most of the seedlings we had brought with us. The site, which the Poles had cleared of brush, was about seventy-five miles outside of Warsaw. There we planted U.S. trees alongside Polish trees for a comparative study of survival, health, growth rates, and so forth.

Jean had a bad cold and fever, so she didn't travel much with me. But she did enjoy visits from a Polish lady in Warsaw, with whom she became friends, while I went with Polish officials to see some government nurseries near the Soviet border. I got to look right across the border into Russia.

After that special, experimental planting, the forestry director who had driven us out to the site, took me aside.

"Frank," he said, "We are going to leave here shortly and go up town, and you are going to ride with me."

We drove about twenty or thirty minutes to a little settlement where my host pulled off the road at a kind of roadhouse or restaurant.

"Frank, we are having a little party for you and your wife," he said. "It's for being nice to Poland and bringing us trees, and coming here to be friendly with us."

Inside the restaurant two long tables had been set up and heaped with food and liquor. Foresters from all around the district were there. As the party got going, the foresters said, "Frank, what are you going to have to drink?"

I said, "I'm sorry, but I don't drink. I'm kinda like, uh, did you ever hear of a prohibitionist?"

They wanted to know what a prohibitionist was and I tried to explain that I didn't care much about drinking hard liquor.

The forestry director hammered on the table. "Frank, in Poland we drink."

"Well, it looks like I'm a captive here in Poland," I

said. "I guess as long as you have a sober driver, I can take a drink."

So they poured me cognac which I sipped from time to time, but drank mostly orange juice. My hosts toasted everything—Polish-American friendship; trees; tree planting; me; Polish-American friendship; the weather; me; themselves. As the party got toastier and louder, one of the foresters said, "Frank, teach us some American songs. We want to learn more about America."

So I had everybody stand in a circle and put their hands on each other's shoulders. And we sang. I taught them a couple of songs and we had a very good time. Everybody got home safely, but I suppose there were some headaches the next morning. The foresters invited me back the next year, but I told them maybe I could return in five years. Now it's been thirteen years, and I haven't been back to visit with them at all.

I suspect the weather destroyed many of the seedlings we planted in Poland. In 1985, northern Europe, including Poland, Norway, Sweden, Denmark, and Finland had the coldest winter ever recorded in that area. Many, many tree seedlings and trees froze completely.

When I got back to the Forum Hotel in Warsaw after my little party, I discovered that Jean was not feeling at all well. The next morning, Sunday, I went down to the desk and asked if they could call an English-speaking doctor. They did. He came, checked Jean, and prescribed some antibiotics for her. His fee was ten dollars—American.

I walked to the fanciest hotel in Warsaw, I can't remember the name, and showed a taxi driver my prescription.

"Take... me... to... a... drug... store." It's funny that you think if you speak slowly enough, the other person will understand even though he doesn't know the language. It worked.

He said, "Yes, yes, yes," and he drove me to the first drugstore he found. I got out and he drove away.

The store was closed. I learned later that just about all drugstores in Warsaw were closed on Sunday. So here I was dumped out on the street, not knowing where I was. I started walking without the slightest idea of where I was going. One office had a sign in the window, "Austrian Travel Service." It was open. I went in and called out, "Hi!" A girl came from a back room, and I told her what I wanted.

"Well I can't speak English much, but I will try to help you."

She began to phone, trying to find an open drugstore. When she finally did, she drew a map for me. I eventually found the place, and gave the pharmacist the prescriptions—there seemed to be three of them. When I returned in a few minutes, there were only two filled. I handed back the unfilled prescription, insisting that it be filled. The pharmacist just laughed and shook his head. I pushed the paper at him again, insisting he fill it. Gridlock. Eventually, a lady who spoke English came into the store. She read the slip of paper and began laughing.

"Do you know what you are trying to do?" she asked me. "You're trying to make the pharmacist make up medicine from a slip of paper with the address of a drugstore the doctor thought might be open today."

While Jean was recovering, I went sightseeing. There were two things I wanted to see—the church in the Wilnow Palace where Jacqueline Kennedy's sister was married, and the changing of the guard at the Tomb of the Unknown Soldier. I hired a cab to take me to the church, but apparently it wasn't as famous as I had assumed, since the cabby couldn't find it. He drove around for almost an hour, then gave up. So he took me back to the hotel, and then didn't want to charge me. I paid him anyway. I went to a newsstand, bought a map of the city, and had the hotel clerk circle the church. Then I tried a cab again, and the next cabby was able to drive right to it. I went inside the church and looked around, finding it all very impressive. I started walking, trying to find the Tomb of the Unknown Soldier. I hadn't the slightest idea where it, or I, was. So I did what I always do in such a situation. I asked.

No matter where you might be, there is always somebody who speaks at least a little English. With good humor, some sign language, and perhaps a map or instructions someone has written down, I have always been able to get from point "A" to "B."

In Warsaw that Sunday, I spotted a family—a couple of children and their parents—out for a stroll. I walked up to them and said, "Hi. How do I find the Tomb of the Unknown Soldier?" I had drawn a blank. None of them spoke English. The man even called his daughter over to listen to me, but she just shrugged. It was time for some body language.

I stood up straight, at attention, and saluted. I marched up and down, pretending to have a gun on my shoulder. That did it. They all laughed. The man took me by the arm and we all walked to the Tomb of the Unknown Soldier, where I got to see the changing of the guard. It was an impressive ritual. My new friends and I parted company with good feelings all around. I suppose they went home and had a good laugh over the crazy American who wasn't afraid to risk making a fool of himself just so he could visit one of Warsaw's landmarks.

During our stay in Warsaw, some of the foresters I had met took Jean and me to an evening at the opera, and Mr. Burzynski, who was our guide, had us over to his home for dinner. We felt awkward eating their food, which, we were sure, was taken from a meager larder. Those were hard times in Poland, so we truly appreciated their thoughtfulness.

Jean and I didn't visit any of the World War II areas where the Germans and Russians had massacred people. We didn't want to see those sites, but you couldn't be in the country without running into reminders of the war. One day when we were walking in the Bialowieza Forest in the eastern part of the country, we came on a monument where several hundred people had been herded together and shot by the Germans. Our guides said that they hadn't even been buried, merely left in the woods for animals or nature to take care of.

The Germans destroyed all the commercial buildings in Warsaw. But about an hour out of Warsaw, there is a magnificent old castle, the only building in Warsaw Hitler ordered to be saved. He planned for it to be his headquarters after he conquered the country.

The night before we left Poland, Mr. Burzynski invited me to his house. He had a tape recorder and asked me to speak into it so he could learn the correct pronunciation of the names of Indian tribes from Washington, and other places. The Snohomish; the Suquamish; the Snoqualmie; the Puyallup; the Hoquiam; the Quillayute; the Issaqualt; the Ennumclaw; I never did learn why.

When we got ready to leave, the Polish foresters gave me seeds to take home for experimental planting. At the airport, the customs officials just waved us on through, not even looking at our baggage, because of the important Polish foresters with us.

A few years later, the U.S. Forest Service needed European larch seeds from areas of Poland, but relations were strained between the two countries, and no cooperative projects were being undertaken. A friend of mine, an employee of the Forest Service, contacted me, asking for help. As a private citizen, I had no political restraints on my reforestation activities, so I wrote to my Polish forester friends with the request. In return for their seeds I offered to furnish them with seeds or trees they needed for their experimentation. This was a good trade all around, and it didn't cost the U.S. taxpayers anything. That kind of service fits nicely into ReTree's goals. Trees don't know anything about national borders.

We have met some of our best international friends through this seed-distribution program. Dr. Peter Tigerstedt, for example, who is Director of Forest Sciences at the University of Helsinki in Finland.

During our trip to Poland, I had met a group of foresters from Finland. Several of them indicated that they would like to have some seeds from Canada, and the United States, especially Alaska and other northern areas. They wanted to do some experimental plantings of trees from different locations, but were lacking seeds. I volunteered ReTree to help.

After returning home, I wrote to these forestry officials, but never got an answer. This one-sided correspondence went on for a long time. Finally I got kind of irked and went to a friend who had a telex machine. I telexed a message to the president of Finland. Within a few days I had an answer that put us into one of our largest projects, certainly *the* largest seed collection.

The Finns sent me a list of tree species they wanted and from where. So I set to work. I was fortunate to have the help of Dr. Sam Foster, a friend and member of ReTree's Board. At the time he was working for the Crown Zellerbach Corporation in their research facility near my home in Wilsonville, and he helped me organize the collecting and cataloging of the seeds.

The collection, which had to be accompanied by detailed information on each tree in it, took more than a year to assemble. I was on the telephone for several hours nearly every morning, trying to reach people and organizations that had seed collections. If the seeds they had were on the list I had from Finland, I asked for them. Almost every organization I asked responded favorably and helped to gather the seeds.

Dr. Tigerstedt had written that they'd like to have some seed from a special place in the Whitehorse, Yukon Territory area, a special kind of larch, for test planting in Lapland. I called the forester in Whitehorse and told him the situation.

"I'll tell you what I'll do" he said. "I'll send you half of what I have, although that's not very much."

In a few days I received the seed.

It didn't seem like much, so I called the fellow in Whitehorse and said, "Lapland is a big area, and this doesn't seem like very much seed for them to work with. How about letting me have the rest of the seed you have? You gave me half. How about giving me all of it?"

There was silence on the line for a moment, then he said, "Well, okay. I guess I can collect some more next year."

He was so generous I really felt kind of ashamed for asking, but I wanted to help those Finnish foresters and scientists. I was touched by his generosity, and by way of thanks, sent him a sack of Oregon filberts.

Gradually, our collection grew. Crown Zellerbach let me use a corner of their storage facility for storing my seed at the proper temperature and humidity. They even gave me access to that room, which was usually off-limits.

Their research facility had thirty-five scientists in it, so I got to meet many of the people who were working in different areas of forest science. One of them was Dr. Jim Lin, who became one of ReTree's directors. After Zellerbach closed the facility, Dr. Lin, the only foreign member of our board, returned to live in Taiwan.

When the collection was complete, it contained seed from six hundred locations in Canada, Alaska, the northeastern United States, and even Korea and China. More than fifty species of trees and shrubs were represented, and it was the largest single collection of tree seed the Finns had ever had.

In 1985, Dr. Tigerstedt called me on the phone and said, "Frank, this season we had the worst storm that Northern Europe has ever seen. We think we lost a lot of our trees. We have some seedling western larch out in our nursery. We brought some of them into the greenhouse to see if they are actually alive and healthy, and it appears that they are. So we're going to have a special tree planting of those seedlings this spring. We want you to come and help us plant them. Those seedlings came from you and were free to help our research, and we feel indebted to you."

I accepted. But I felt that the Canadians whose response had been almost one hundred percent—should also be represented. I called the Canadian ambassador to Finland. He was at lunch, but just as I was about to hang up, he picked up the phone. I told him the story and invited him to the planting. He said to come by or phone when we got to Finland.

I invited Lorne Wheelon, with whom I had been friends

since our Scouting days, to go to Finland with me, and when we got to Finland we went to the Canadian embassy. The ambassador said he'd come to the planting and bring some people, which he did. Once there, he insisted on planting trees with Lorne and me.

The Finns made us feel very welcome. And after we planted the larch, they took us to visit some of their forest research facilities, and to travel along the Russian border, where we saw watchtowers just across the line. They seemed very threatening. When we drove along certain places in range of the towers, a Finnish official would time our departure. I guess if we hadn't made it to the next checkpoint by a certain time, they'd have sent somebody out to check on us.

Many of the seeds we collected are in storage, so the Finnish foresters will be able to draw on the collection for years.

Chapter 17

...[O]ut of the ground made the Lord God to grow every tree that is pleasant to the sight and good for food; the tree of life also in the midst of the garden, and the tree of the knowledge of good and evil... And the Lord God commanded the man, saying, "Of every tree of the garden thou mayest freely eat: But of the tree of the knowledge of good and evil, thou shalt not eat of it..."

—Genesis 2:9

Ever since Adam took that first bite of an apple, trees have been an important part of human myth and folklore. They probably figured in the tales that storytellers used to pass along history. They have been used to tell us, in parable, about what it means to be human. Because of the long relationship we humans have had with trees, this is understandable.

If we read the fossil records correctly, about sixty million years ago, a small mammal that looked much like today's tree shrew scurried aloft into the trees. Why? Maybe to escape danger; maybe to find food. In any event, it didn't leave. The tree was a source of food—leaves, bark, blossoms, insects, small birds. The tree was a sanctuary. The big predators on the ground couldn't reach the little mammal, and by snuggling deep among the leaves, it was secure from those that dropped out of the sky. As long as it didn't fall, it was safe.

By taking up housekeeping in the tree, the creature made some significant physical changes that took millions of years.

The clawed digits on its paws evolved into hands and

feet with flattened nails. Now the little mammal could grab a branch rather than having to dig into it. It could hold on with one hand, and reach for food with the other. It could hold its baby while moving through the trees. "Treads" developed to give the fingers and toes more traction.

Now that it had a solid grip on its new home, the mammal needed to know exactly *where* to grab. It needed depth perception. The animal already had a pair of eyes. They were just in the wrong place—on the sides of its head. For life on the ground, that was fine. They gave vision up, sideways and somewhat to the rear. Who knows where a predator might come from? But the eye placement didn't provide depth perception. So they moved. Over hundreds of thousands of years, they shifted forward until they were side by side on the animal's face, just far enough apart so that each eye had a slightly different view of the world. The result was binocular vision—depth perception.

Equipped with hands and feet that could grab and eyes that told it where to grab, all the creature needed was some mechanism that could process the information the eyes gave and send it to the hands and feet. It needed a better brain than it had. It already owned the most highly developed one in the animal kingdom. With a little more development, mainly in the prefrontal lobes, the adaptation to arboreal life was pretty well complete.

Other physical changes came along over time, as though in anticipation of that final drop from the tree onto the ground. The animal became more adept at balancing itself on its hind legs. And gradually its pelvic area changed its configuration. Its head tilted back on the neck. Its feet swung ninety degrees at the ankle, making the animal flat-footed.

The changes were slow, unbelievably slow, and they occurred in more than one species of primate. Approximately two or three million years ago, the creature that carried the successful changes, dropped from the trees and took up terrestrial life.

Why?

Nobody knows for sure, but there are hints. About twelve million years ago, the earth experienced an eons-long series of droughts. Forests dried up and died. Our ancestors had to drop from the trees and head out onto the grasslands if they wanted to eat.

There is another possibility, or perhaps it complements the drought theory.

The discipline of ecology indicates that there are "niches" in the world's ecosystems. That is, there are countless conditions like temperature, humidity, soil type, food availability, the kinds of food available, the presence or absence of predators. Each one of these can accommodate only certain types of life forms. Further, there is the argument that where an ecological niche exists, there is also a life form, or one that will evolve, to fit into it.

A few million years ago, there was an ecological niche for a ground-dwelling, bipedal, fairly intelligent animal. Our proto-human ancestor fit into it.

It didn't seem a likely candidate. Small, naked, without fangs, not able to outrun most of the animals that wanted to eat it, nor those it wanted to eat.

But all those millennia in the trees paid off. Its hands and feet, binocular vision, magnificent brain, and bipedal stance were ready-made features for terrestrial life.

The primate species, *homo sapiens*, eventually came to control the entire world, but it also gradually moved away from the intimate relationship it had had with nature. It became essentially a creature of the city. Yet locked deep inside it there exists a memory of those days when home meant trees. It often surfaces in our myths and folklore.

In the psychology that is peculiarly human, trees have taken on meanings that go beyond objective reality.

Trees as symbols must have developed early on in the human mind. With their heavy trunks and outstretched branches, trees must have seemed another form of human, even superhuman. They were so large, so long-lived—immortal when seen from the human time frame—perhaps they were messengers of the gods. Maybe they *were* gods.

As early man pondered the ultimate questions of existence—Who am I, where did I come from, where am I going?—he often used trees as metaphors for the answers.

When humans got around to pondering the question of good and evil, the tree became a convenient symbol.

In his book, *The Triumph of the Tree*, John Stewart Collis comments on "…the forbidden tree through which we were expelled from the paradise of innocent ignorance, and took upon ourselves the burden of understanding."

Psychologically, in order to develop consciousness, humanity had to take that first bite of knowledge. There is no place to go (or grow) in Paradise.

But awareness exacts a price. It's called a reality check.

The legend of the tree of life and of good and evil, even of creation and Eden, predates the Old Testament. An ancient Persian myth places the first man and woman in Heden, the Garden of Paradise, where they eat a forbidden fruit and are driven out into the world. In Sumer, about 3,000 B.C., a tree was part of the creation myth. In Irish myth the first man was created from an alder; his wife, from a mountain ash. In Rome, the oak tree was man's mother, and she nourished him with her acorns. A Scandinavian myth tells how Odin created the first man and woman from two trees growing on the beach.

If humans can be created from trees in myth, they can just as easily be turned back. In a Greek myth, two poor peasants, Bacuis and his wife, Philemon, are deeply devoted, and pray that one does not outlive the other. One day, they befriend Zeus and Hermes who are passing through, disguised as mortals. In gratitude, the gods convert the peasants' cottage into a temple overseen by the man and his wife. Years later, when death approaches, the humans embrace and say goodbye. But the gods remember their prayer for togetherness and enclose them in a great tree whose intertwined branches assure they will never be separated.

To the weavers of myth and legend, the tree bestowed knowledge, wisdom, bliss, and courage. It was the ladder on which the dead could mount to Heaven. It provided milk, water, dew, rain; its juices were intoxicating; its seed was the force from which life was formed; its trunk was the home of the gods; its roots reached into the underworld where springs rose to water the rivers of the world; its branches held up sky; its leaves were clouds; its fruit, stars.

According to a Scandinavian myth, the world is flat, and at its center grows the Tree of Life, Yggdrasil. Its branches cover the world; its leaves drip honey and other food. It has three roots, one in the underworld, another in this world, the third in heaven. They are cared for by the Fates—Past, Present and Future—who water them from sacred fountains. An eagle sits in the tree's top, and a dragon gnaws at its roots, trying to destroy the order of creation. A little squirrel runs up and down the tree trunk, carrying messages back and forth from crown to roots, beneath which the horn of doom lies. When this sounds, the tree will split open, the seas will rise, and the god of fire will burn up the world. But from the ashes will rise another, better universe, with an ash tree at its center.

The Yggdrasil legend is repeated almost word for word in a Persian creation myth. Yet, so far as we know, there was no contact between ancient Persia and Scandinavia. But it should come as no surprise that human myths are much the same wherever they originate. We are all human, with much the same concerns; our myths are attempts to answer them.

As the ages passed, forests changed from being dark, unknown places filled with danger to rather pleasant places.

In Greece, Pan—half-goat, half-man—appeared, as god of the woods. He was pictured wearing a fir wreath, holding a tree branch in one hand, and standing beside an oak or pine. A mischief maker, he sometimes tricked humans, but more often helped them by protecting their flocks. By and large, he spent his time playing the pipes and cavorting with nymphs and satyrs in the woods.

The nymphs were goddesses in ancient Greece.

Dryads—wood spirits—took their name from the Greek word for tree, *drus*. They lived in trees, groves and forests. One group, the Hamadryads, had long, flowing hair and carried axes with which they protected their trees. These demigods were female humans down to the waist, with tree trunks for lower bodies. They were virgins, and it was important that they protect their trees because they died on the tree with which they were associated. Linden, willow, and pomegranate trees are named for Hamadryads.

In mythology, apples are the supreme fruit. The Latin name for the apple, *pumila*, is taken from Pomona, the Greek goddess of all fruit trees. When Hercules was assigned twelve labors, retrieval of the golden apples Juno had given to Jupiter as a wedding gift was one of them.

Druids revered the apple tree because they believed that only on it and the oak could sacred mistletoe grow.

The oak is one of the best-known trees throughout the northern temperate zone, where many of its three hundred species grow, and one of the most impressive trees in the forest. Some grow more than a hundred feet tall, spread their branches 150 feet, and live for hundreds of years. A mature oak stands deep-rooted in the earth, gnarled and rugged, with massive branches that scoff at the laws of gravity. Let other trees bow to the passing wind, the oak digs in, hunching its massive shoulders against the worst that nature can throw at it.

Any oak, so long as it had mistletoe growing in it, was assumed to be the home of Thunar—the Teutonic thunder god. Mistletoe came from heaven, riding a lightning bolt, and lodged in the tree. It needed no roots in the earth, but hid among the branches and derived its sustenance from Thunar's tree itself. When the tree "died" each autumn, its life passed into the mistletoe, which stayed green year-round.

Groves of oak trees were often temples. Priests called Druids—men of the oak—conducted religious services in them, slaughtering the finest bulls to placate their deities. They cut mistletoe from the trees and distributed pieces to the people as charms. Mistletoe was used as bandage and healing for wounds, an antidote for poison, and a cure for diseases, among them epilepsy. It was so important that dropping the mistletoe on the ground was considered a sacrilege.

In Greece the oak was the tree of Zeus, and his sanctuary at Dodona was the god's earthly home. It is said that there are more thunderstorms there than in any other place in Europe. The Greeks believed that the oak was the first tree on earth and that Zeus's cradle hung from its branches.

In Rome, Zeus was replaced by Jupiter, but the oak remained his royal tree. Roman kings claimed to be representatives of Jupiter. The poet Virgil depicted these Silvii (wood) kings as crowned with wreaths of oak leaves, so an oak wreath became a symbol of the highest honor, the ultimate tribute.

In both Greece and Rome, oak groves were holy places, where the gods came to dispense wisdom and prophecy. Oracles were the mediums used by the gods to speak to the people through the rustling of leaves and swaying of branches.

Inevitably the practice clashed head-on with the teachings of Judaism and Christianity. God ordered Moses to...

"[D]estroy their... [the pagans']... altars, break their images, and cut down their groves."

Exodus 34:13

Of the 41 references to groves in the Old Testament, 40 are negative.

In 719 A.D., Pope Gregory II sent Wynfrith Boniface to Germany to convert the pagans. One of his first actions was to order Odin's sacred oaks felled. The people were aghast. They warned Boniface that he was playing with fire—divine fire—that would come streaking down from heaven and torch him.

"Never fear," Boniface said in effect. "The true God is here," and he ordered the trees cut. Lightning did not strike. Odin was dead.

Boniface recognized that the people needed a symbol

to replace the fallen oaks, and there was one conveniently at hand. The fir tree was considered immortal because it seemed to live on in winter when other trees "died." Legend has it that Boniface dedicated the fir to the Holy Child, and everybody was happy. Everybody except Odin.

A German legend says that, in the sixteenth century, Martin Luther saw a small, snow-covered fir tree glistening in the moonlight one Christmas Eve. He cut it and took it home for his children, and it became the first Christmas tree.

Trees figure heavily in legends which developed around the cross on which Christ was crucified.

In one, Adam, at age nine hundred years, sensed the approach of his death. He sent his son, Seth, to ask the angel guarding the gate to Paradise for a vial of ambrosia— the Oil of Mercy—from the Tree of Life. With it, Adam could anoint his limbs and regain good health. Seth found a young man, radiant as the sun, sitting on top of the tree. The youth introduced himself as the Son of God who would come to earth in the future to deliver it from sin. He said he would not give the Oil of Mercy for Adam, but gave Seth three seeds from the Tree of Life, which were to be put in Adam's mouth after he died. Seth obeyed. The seeds grew into three saplings of olive, cedar, and cypress. Their existence was unknown until the time of Moses, who was ordered by God to cut three rods from them. With these rods, Moses performed many miracles. After his death, they were lost until King David recovered them. Before David died, he tossed the rods into a cistern, where they took root and grew as one tree, the wood of which eventually was made into the cross.

An Austrian version of this legend says that the Angel Michael gave Eve and her son, Seth, a spray with three leaves from the Tree of Knowledge, and directed them to plant it on Adam's grave. It became the tree which Solomon used to build the first Temple, and eventually became wood for the cross.

In a German version, Noah saved Eve's tree from the flood. When the dove which he sent out brought back a sprig of olive, Noah planted it alongside the trees he had saved, and it became wood for the cross.

As today's three main religions, Christianity, Judaism, and Islam replaced the old gods, tree legends shifted from being almost entirely metaphors and parables with a religious focus—to folklore.

The use of tree limbs to "witch" for water is as old as the belief in magic. Present-day practitioners disclaim any supernatural involvement.

A water witch we have hereabout insists that the pull is so strong it will peel the bark off the forked wand in his hands.

After oaks gave up their position as religious symbols, they still maintained their status in folklore.

In the 17th century, King Charles II returned from exile to overthrow Oliver Cromwell and his Roundheads. The king was defeated in the battle of Worcester on September 3, 1651. He and an aide escaped from Cromwell's army by hiding in an oak tree, which became known as the "Royal Oak." The tree is long gone, but in front of many an English inn swings a sign with the royal oak painted on it. His Majesty can be spotted peeking out from among the branches.

In 1687, Connecticut's Governor, Sir Edmund Andros, tried to steal the colony's charter for his own political purposes. Joseph Wadsworth supposedly hid it in the cleft of an oak tree. More than a century later, when a storm felled the tree, church bells tolled its passing. Its wood was fashioned into picture frames, ceremonial gavels, and several chairs, one of which, called the "Governor's Chair," is on exhibit in the museum of the Connecticut Historical Society.

We in America have a couple of tree legends, one of which is factual.

In the early 1800s, a nurseryman named John Chapman worked his way across the lake states. He was quite an eccentric, noted for wearing strange clothes and holding nontraditional religious beliefs. He was kind to animals and dedicated to planting apple trees. By the time he died in 1845, John Chapman was already a legend called Johnny Appleseed. Some of my friends call me a latter-day Johnny Appleseed. And because I involve children in my tree planting, they also say I'm a Pied Piper. That's a nice mixture.

Probably the best-known American tree hero was a logger. Paul Bunyan was vaguely known in logging camps before the turn of this century, but it was an advertising man, W. B. Laughead, who presented Paul to the general public.

Paul was taller than the tallest fir, stronger than one hundred men, so big he used a charred pine tree as a pencil and brushed his beard with a fully grown spruce. They say Paul was a French-Canadian, and that when he stepped across the border into the United States, he lost his accent and changed the spelling of his name from the French, Bunyon, to "Bunyan." He had a pet ox named Babe, who measured forty-two axe handles and a plug of tobacco between the horns. Babe showed up in camp during the Winter of the Blue Snow, when the temperature dropped so low the snow turned blue from the cold.

Paul and Babe dug the St. Lawrence River so people would know when they were in Canada or the United States, then plowed out the Grand Canyon and Puget Sound. Old-time loggers still talk about the fight Paul had with Hels Helsen, the Wild Bull of the Woods. The dust they raised piled up to become the Black Hills. Poor Babe came to a bad end. One day he ate too many of the pancakes that Paul's three hundred flapjack cooks made each morning, and died of the world's biggest bellyache.

The word among loggers is that Paul is living somewhere in the Pacific Northwest woods, and that on windy days you can hear him brushing his beard with a spruce tree.

Chapter 18

There is magic in planting a tree. I sometimes think that placing the seedling in a hole you have dug in the good, rich soil is like handling the tree's spirit. We all share this spirit; it is like a thread that binds us together. The naturalist, John Muir, once wrote, "When we try to pick out anything by itself, we find it hitched to everything else in the universe."

In our modern civilization, so far removed from the natural world, we tend to forget this spirit that all life has in common. But I also think that it is so old, coming from our very first days on earth, that we can't completely forget, or neglect it. It is always there, somewhere below the surface of our lives, ready to pop up under the right stimulus. Trees have a magic.

One of my associates in ReTree owns forty acres in Oregon, on which grow a few dozen Douglas fir trees. They're all second growth of course, because just about all the region where my friend lives was logged around the turn of the century. But these trees are very impressive. Most of them are more than one hundred feet tall, and upwards of two feet in diameter. My friend loves those trees.

Recently one of them went down in an especially heavy storm, and my friend told me that it was as though he had lost a child. That magnificent tree was lying there on the hill, down on the ground. I suppose most people aren't this sentimental about trees, but I'm sure there is something in that tree spirit.

If so, it's understandable that people respond to somebody like me, who goes around the world planting trees. Maybe people think the magic is in the person, rather than the trees. Well, that's all right; the important thing is to get the trees planted.

A few years ago, we were in the Dominican Republic planting trees. After the tree planting, Ralph Hannan, my associate in ReTree and a long-term friend, decided we should take a walk along the beach in Santo Domingo.

This beach front is open to the public for maybe twelve or fifteen miles, so Ralph and I decided to walk along it and enjoy the evening. After a few minutes, two pretty girls came along and began walking with us. (Of course, the prettiest one walked with me.) Well, we might be from Oregon, but we didn't just fall off the turnip wagon. We knew what they wanted. They were poor ladies who made their living doing favors for men, and they let us know their bodies were available, for a small charge, or a huge charge for that matter. They kept walking along with us, trying to make a deal. They said there was a car following them and we could all go to their home in it.

After a while Ralph said, "Frank, these young ladies have been working pretty hard. I think they've earned some money."

"Good," I said. "Let's pay them. Then maybe we'd better get back to our wives. They're expecting us and will be very suspicious if we don't show up on time. But we are interested. Maybe tomorrow we can see each other."

So we gave them each a couple of dollars and said that we appreciated their offer to be good friends. Of course, that was the last we saw of them. We didn't have our wives with us in Santo Domingo, and we didn't go back to the beach.

The following day we went to the airport to catch our plane. We were headed for Haiti next, but for some reason, had to go back to Miami first. It didn't seem to make much sense, since the Dominican Republic and Haiti sit, cheek to jowl, on the small island of Hispaniola. Maybe it was a matter of politics. Papa Doc Duvalier was in control of Haiti in those days, and Batista was the dictator in the Dominican Republic. Maybe they didn't like each other.

Ralph and I went to the Santo Domingo airport early, got our tickets, and went to the gate to wait. Our flight was announced as leaving Santo Domingo at 9:00 a.m. Ralph got into the book he was reading and I kind of kept an eye on the gate. When nine o'clock approached, they still hadn't announced our flight, so I went to the ticket counter.

"What's up?" I asked. "Our ticket says gate number 4; we're supposed to leave in a few minutes and our plane hasn't been announced."

The guy said, "Oh, that is the wrong gate. Your plane left from gate six half an hour ago. You'll have to wait here in the airport until tomorrow."

"Oh, no, I don't have to wait here in the airport until tomorrow. We bought a ticket in good faith, and you accepted our money, and it's up to you. It's your duty to get us to Miami."

The manager came down. I explained we were in the Dominican Republic to plant trees to help the country's future forests and now had to get to Miami to make connections for the next tree planting.

"Tree planting," he said. "Hmm. It is true. We have wronged you and we're going to see what we can do."

He was as good as his word. At one o'clock we were on a plane bound for Miami, riding in first class.

Two of my neighbors on the plane were a woman and her husband. I started talking to the lady and told her why we were there in the Dominican Republic.

"That's wonderful," she said. "My interest is in the environment and getting tree planting done also."

I gave her our brochure, which solicits contributions, and she put an "X" in the one thousand dollar square. I promised that if she gave this amount, we would guarantee to spend the money on projects in the Dominican Republic. Later, in Miami, she and her husband helped us get through the terminal to make connections with our plane to Haiti.

You just never know where the tree spirit will strike. It might be on a beach in Santo Domingo or in a plane flying thirty-five thousand feet above the Caribbean.

I'm a few years older than Ralph Hannan who often travels with me, and he sees taking care of me as one of his assignments.

On that trip to the Caribbean region, he said, "Frank, just to help out, I think I'll take care of our passports and our tickets." I guess he thought maybe this old guy was losing his marbles and needed somebody to care for him.

As soon as we got on the plane at Panama City, Ralph buried his face in a book about Peter the Great or Frederick the Great. One of the Greats, anyway. As for me, I did as I was told; I handed him my passport and ticket. After we got off in Miami and were planning to take a flight to Puerto Rico, Ralph came to me.

"Frank, I don't know where your ticket and passport are."

We got ahold of Eastern Airlines and asked if the plane was still on the ground. They said it had already gone, so the only thing we could do was to go to the Eastern office, report the ticket missing, get another one, and catch the flight to Puerto Rico. I didn't need a passport to enter there, but I had to buy another ticket, and when I got home, there would be the matter of the passport to take care of.

I've been to Haiti three times. In 1986 I went there with Hinkey Foleen. Like Ralph Hannan, Hinkey spent a lot of time in a book about one or the other of the Greats.

In Port au Prince, the country's capital, we sought out the best hotel, figuring that the best might be none too good. We found one which had a pool. However, we didn't take advantage of it, since the water looked a little too rich. The concept of twentieth-century sanitation hasn't quite reached parts of Haiti yet, so we also opted for showers rather than tubs while we were there.

We got to visit with the U.S. embassy people and officials of CARE and US AID. I've never had bad experiences with any of these three groups. Agricultural attachés in the embassies seem to go out of their way to help; and CARE and AID are more or less in the same business as we are—trying to help the local people.

As soon as we were settled in the hotel, I called the local Lions Club. We had already made plans to cosponsor a tree planting with schoolchildren, so a couple of their representatives met with us to firm up the event. We agreed to plant at a certain school, using some of the students and some Boy Scouts and Girl Scouts. The Lions told us they had a project underway at that school—to furnish running water and sanitary toilets. I said that for their help with the tree planting, I would ask my Lions Club in Oregon to contribute a couple of hundred American dollars to the projects. When I got back home and told the club members there were three hundred children without running water or sanitary toilets, the club didn't give the Haitian Lions two hundred dollars. They gave five hundred.

Haiti is probably the worst example of what can happen when a land is deforested. The island is hilly, and with its tree cover gone, erosion is a major problem. I have never seen such an ecological disaster. When Columbus came to the new world, he found island after island in the Caribbean covered with thick, healthy forests. On Hispaniola, he wrote in his journal that a person had a hard time getting through the lush growths of trees. But a little later, when the Europeans introduced sugar cane into the area, they began cutting the forests for the firewood they needed to boil down the raw cane. In less than one century, the forests were reduced to isolated clumps of trees.

Haiti also suffers from overgrazing by cows and goats, especially goats. These horned locusts not only eat the ground cover down to its roots, but they also destroy the soil. Their tiny hoofs pulverize it, killing whatever roots are left, and opening it to wind and water. The soil of Haiti is lying on the bottom of the Caribbean.

Our government is spending lots of money there on

tree-planting projects. They want to plant billions of trees in Haiti. Some U.S. agencies are giving Haitian farmers trees to plant each year and crediting them for planting them. But the country is so badly eroded, I don't know if the efforts to replant it are gaining or not. If the trees do get planted and the livestock leave them alone, and there is enough soil for them to grow, they still face a bleak future. Often, when trees get a couple of inches in diameter, people hack them off, carry them to the city and sell them for charcoal. Most of the people are desperately poor, and poor people will cut trees anywhere to sustain their lives. They'll feel particularly free to cut trees on public land because they think that any land that belongs to the government is theirs.

Near our hotel, I saw a lady with a child, and asked her as best I could if I could take a picture of her and the child. She nodded, so I pinned one of ReTree's little tree badges on their blouses, then took the picture. I guess she thought I would pay her, but I didn't understand this, and walked away. She started after me to get some money. Everybody had told me not to give people money but she kept following me for an hour or so, before leaving. Then as I was coming back up to the hotel, she appeared again, so I gave her a dollar. That dollar was about one week's wages for a Haitian.

After the tree planting that year, we returned a couple more times to Haiti. The last time I went, a young man named Daniel Groschong from Oregon went with me to serve as the project's photographer and scribe. I try to take notes and photos of each of our projects. These days, I've added video. It seems important to keep a record of these events, and the local groups who participate enjoy getting back a few pictures, or, ideally a video.

Daniel and I held our tree planting in an area outside of Port au Prince near the school that the Lions were helping. Three hundred children attended the school where we planted local trees and a few we had brought for experimental planting—a few giant sequoias and coast redwoods from California.

Of course I wanted to get the children in a picture. There were three hundred of them, all about the same age and all lined up. One little boy had just a shirt on, with no shorts. I was going to take his picture, but decided it wouldn't be proper, that they might think I was belittling him. But none of the other children paid any attention to it at all.

Before the event, we had arranged with U.S. AID to furnish little avocado trees in containers and we gave each child one of these with instructions to plant it at home. I was supposed to come back in two or three years to check on the trees, and maybe give a prize of some kind to the child whose care had resulted in the best tree. But I've never been back.

Whether I'll ever go back, I don't know. I suppose some time I will. But I'm a little scared of the sanitation situation there, and until the present political situation is straightened out, I just don't know how welcome an American, even one with nothing more lethal than baby trees in his pack, would be. Not that I ever had any trouble. The people were very nice and helpful. The forestry people were always willing to help.

But there always seems to be the threat of trouble in the country. During one of my trips, soldiers were marching around and there were tanks and so forth. We were told that the airport was closed, so I went to the American embassy to find out what the situation really was. They said they didn't think the airport was closed, and advised us simply to go there. We found a taxi and in spite of people in the town who were trying to blockade the highway, we caught our flight out.

Another thing that might keep me from going back to Haiti is the amount of walking a person has to do to get around. The country is very hilly, and my poor old hips are beginning to rebel at the tasks I assign to them. One of them has already been replaced with plastic or stainless steel or something.

So I don't know about Haiti.

About 1985 I learned that the world forestry conference, which I think is held every three or four years, would be in Mexico City. I called the world forestry headquarters, asked about registering for the conference, and told them we would like to have an exhibit. They said that exhibits were accepted and that I could arrange for it at the time of my arrival. I went to the conference, taking with me Sanford Yates, a forester with the Mt. Hood National Forest, who is in charge of construction in the forest, building trails and structures for visitors.

Sanford and I flew to Mexico City and registered for the conference. One of the first people I met there was David Harcharik, who is now Director of International Forestry for the U.S. Forest Service. With him was Mr. Little, a librarian and archivist with the service.

I brought along my exhibit, which was pretty simple. The signs read something like, "The forests of the world are disappearing at an alarming rate. Every possible inch of land worldwide should be put back to growing trees. There is nothing so dangerous to the future of the world and its living creatures as the destruction of the forests. We need them for everyone's health." It showed parts of some of our tree plantings on Mt. St. Helens, and invited conference attendees to participate in a tree planting we had scheduled near the city of Puebla. Well, somebody told me that all the regular exhibit space was taken and that no exhibits were permitted in the hallway. But I found a table in the hallway and set up my exhibit. The conference had hired about two dozen pretty Mexican girls, college students, to serve as ushers and receptionists, and I'd made friends with several of them. When the time came to set up my little exhibit, they helped me. We had plenty of space to work in, as the hallway was deserted. Everybody was in the conference auditorium listening to the president of Mexico.

Because I didn't want to sit out there by myself, I asked an usher if I might go in to hear the president talk. He said no seats were available on the main floor, and I would have to go upstairs. I told him it bothered my back to climb stairs, so maybe I would just wait outside. He was a nice person, and came back in a couple of minutes to tell me he had found a seat on the main floor. I went in and sat down next to a forester from Africa. During a break, he managed to convey that he did not speak English. French okay, English no. I said that my English wasn't much good either, and that maybe French would be our chance to get acquainted. We did sort of understand each other. After the speech, he and I walked to a restaurant and had a nice lunch.

When I got back to the hall, my exhibit was gone.

My college girls were just as surprised as I. I went to the garbage and there it was, crushed and torn. I decided that I couldn't let this happen, so I carried the pieces back inside and started assembling the exhibit as best I could, with the help of the girls. They got some paper and wrote in Spanish the time of the following day's tree planting. I figured I was going to have trouble with the exhibit, and sure enough, five men came along, bellowing like bulls.

They surrounded me, shaking their fingers and saying, "You take this exhibit down. No exhibits in the hallway."

I said, "You boys keep your hands off my exhibit. If you put one hand on me or my exhibit, you'll first have to return my $250. Then we'll go to the *policia*. If the *policia* tell me to leave, I'll leave."

They went away shaking their heads, probably talking about the *loco Norte Americano*. Later one of the conference officials came and talked to me. I told him that I had paid my fee, and I needed a place to exhibit; I had found this one, and I expected to keep it. In fact I was going to stay right there and guard it. If I had to leave, the girls would watch it for me.

The exhibit stayed.

In a short time, we had more than enough signatures for the tree planting. Then I disassembled the exhibit, kept the parts I wanted, and took the rest back to the dumpster.

A few years earlier, in Oregon, we had met a Mexican forester named Francisco Ruez (Paco for short). He was studying at the School of Forestry at Oregon State University, and when we mentioned attending the forestry conference, he invited us to do some experimental plantings on his ranch near Puebla. He would get the children and trees if I would furnish foresters from the conference.

The event went off quite well. We had a couple of dozen foresters attend as well as the children Paco got together. Most of the foresters were from Africa.

In Oregon, Paco had studied forestry management to help him in the stewardship of his own forest, which was about a thousand acres. He had many problems, particularly neighbors who were encroaching on his forest land. They set fire to trees on the fringes to kill the little trees so there would be more grass for their cattle. They burned approximately a hectare of land (roughly two and one-half acres) killing all the trees, so they could plow and harrow and disc the land, maybe at night, and plant corn before Paco could discover the intrusion and stop it. The law allowed them to grow, harvest, and keep that crop, even though it was raised on someone else's land. The government even furnished the seed corn free, and when the crop came in, bought it.

Paco said he didn't know how to counter this kind of destruction of his forest. I suggested that we make friends with the schoolchildren in the surrounding area and invite them to a big tree planting on his property. We would give them the biggest feed they'd ever had—hamburgers, ice cream, popcorn, hot dogs, the works. We'd make it a family affair with parents, children, babies, grandparents. "I'll bet you there will not be any more destruction of your land. The children will prevent encroachment on the land of the friend who gave them the biggest party they ever had."

So when I got to Mexico, that is what we did. We had an enormous tree planting, with all the goodies afterward. I hope the plan worked.

About 1984, at a meeting with Dr. John Gordon, then the forest research director at Oregon State University, and Dr. Miguel Espanoza from Chile, I met Miguel Capo Ortega at Oregon State University.

During his time in the graduate program at OSU, my wife and I invited him to our home several times, and we became friends. Eventually he got his doctorate and returned to Saltillo to teach. At about that same time, Crown Zellerbach Corporation sold their holdings to a British firm, and some of my friends who worked there donated the company library to ReTree. We offered the books to Dr. Capo for the library in his new forestry department at Saltillo.

I stayed in touch with my friend and later suggested that his university and ReTree sponsor a tree planting in the mountains near Saltillo. Dr. Capo thought this a good idea, so after one of our tree plantings in Costa Rica, Panama, Honduras, and Guatemala, we traveled home via Saltillo. There we met with Dr. Capo and had a very successful tree planting in association with the university.

Because ReTree has a deep interest in worldwide tree planting, we stay in touch with government officials who have the same involvement. In this way we became acquainted with the Executive Director of International Forestry for the U.S. Forest Service. Recently, I called him and asked if there were some way the service could help with reforestation in the tropics. He referred me to Doug Kneeland, and in 1992 I contacted Mr. Kneeland with a proposal that we return to Saltillo and plant trees with schoolchildren. We also asked that Forest Service foresters Rocky Pancratz and his wife Darci accompany us. Rocky was on firefighting duty in Idaho, so Darci was the only representative of the Forest Service.

We flew down to Saltillo in late August 1992. Our party consisted of Darci, photographer Allan de Lay, my son John, who is studying forestry, and me. Dr. Capo picked us up at the airport and took us on a tour of the planting site.

Saltillo and the surrounding region are in the Sierra de Artigua, a range in the Sierra Madre Oriental. On the highway, we were between eight and nine thousand feet in elevation, and the peaks in the background were close to twelve thousand feet. In the valleys of this area there are apple orchards for miles and miles. All the apple trees in these orchards are covered by a perforated vinyl sheeting—whose purpose is to protect the fruit from hail. I don't have statistics, but I would say this valley must produce most of the apples grown in Mexico.

After dinner that day, we visited an area near Saltillo that looks like the badlands of North and South Dakota— very much the same kind of erosion exists, although on a much smaller scale. There is another difference between the two: The Dakota badlands were the result of natural actions; those near Saltillo were caused by war. At least, that's what I was told.

According to the story, trenches were dug by the Mexicans to slow the advance of the American army during the Mexican-American war of 1848. Over the years, rain and wind have eroded these trenches into the grotesque forms we saw there that summer evening. I find it hard to believe that a few trenches could be the cause of so much damage. But they might be right. We humans have certainly been the cause of tremendous damage to the earth. A look at old photos of former tobacco farms in the American South or deep plowing in the Great Plains will show what can happen when the natural ground cover is disturbed. Those southern farms ended up looking like miniature Dakota badlands. And during the early 1930s, tens of thousands of tons of the finest topsoil in the world was blown off the Great Plains and ended up in the Gulf of Mexico. I don't know how or if the former tobacco farmlands were regenerated. So I suppose soldiers digging trenches in the dry soil near Saltillo could have started a process that resulted in the erosion I saw.

At Saltillo, we planted piñon pine and spruce trees in a mountainous area managed by the university. I asked my friend, Dr. Capo, to make sure the planting area was secure from livestock, and he assured me it would be.

In that area, the farmers plant prickly pear cactus around

their homes to serve as living fences, and to provide fruit. I understand ocotillo cactus is also planted as a fence in the desert parts of northern Mexico where the plant grows naturally. When I saw the prickly pear being used this way, I remembered the oak fence posts that my father and older brothers used to set in the ground. Once in a while, they would sprout. I wonder if those oaks grew and are still standing near that little farm near Sheridan, Oregon.

The local Lions Club at Saltillo was a great help in this planting. They had more than forty people there—many of their members as well as young teenage boys and girls. They furnished tools and labor, and did a fabulous job serving refreshments. The Boy Scouts and Girl Scouts also brought refreshments so everyone had a good feed and a good outing. I think we had six hundred forestry seedlings to plant. I don't know if we got them all planted, but I'm sure the university students went back to take care of any leftovers.

After the tree planting, we suggested to Dr. Capo that in May 1993, we have a planting farther south of the university in the tropics.

In fact, the 1993 project became larger than we had anticipated. In partnership with the U.S. Forest Service, we planted trees in fourteen Central American and Caribbean countries, and prospects are that this cooperative effort will continue in the tropics throughout the world.

Chapter 19

After the conference and tree planting in Mexico City, Sanford Yates and I planned to go to Costa Rica to do a tree planting there with a service club. All the arrangements had been made with the forestry department, and, I thought, one of the local clubs. I had phoned them before leaving Oregon, inviting them to be a partner in this project. They hemmed and hawed, and reluctantly agreed to participate. But when I got in touch in Costa Rica, I discovered they had left a message for me back in Oregon, canceling out. So it appeared Sanford and I were stuck until I contacted the Lions Club.

I called them and found out they were going to have a meeting that evening. The club president invited me and Gilberto Brooks Johnson, a forester with the Costa Rica Department of Natural Resources, to attend.

I told the club president, "I'd like to meet with you and talk about a proposal I have. Maybe I could take you to lunch."

"I don't speak good English," the president said.

"I don't speak very good English either. We'll get along fine," I said.

That evening the Lions were all very excited about participating in the tree planting. But we didn't have much time; it was already Tuesday and the tree planting was scheduled for Saturday. The people at the U.S. Embassy were great.

We got trees from the Forestry Department, and I called the local bishop of the Roman Catholic church, who helped me arrange for everybody to meet at the church. I figured that if there was any place in San José that everybody knew, it would be that church. Buses came, children came.

We planted at about ten thousand feet above sea level, at which elevation trees grow very well in the tropics. There are truck farms high on the side of Mt. Fusio—a volcano—which erupted during a visit by President Kennedy, and the farmers grow beautiful potatoes, carrots, beets, and all kinds of vegetables. Because the site is so high, it doesn't have the stifling heat one has to endure at lower elevations. Yet, because it is in the tropics, it seldom has snow or frost.

It was a tremendous tree planting. Lions showed up in big numbers, as did lots of Scouts. Costa Rica is trying very hard to save its tropical rain forests: Large tracts of forest have been set aside for preservation, and the people are being educated about the importance of the trees with which they have been blessed. As a result, the country is an outstanding example of what can happen when the government and the population of a country decide to save their forests.

We have conducted several tree plantings in Costa Rica, and have always been met with warmth and enthusiasm by the people. The first came about because of a program initiated by President Kennedy called the Friends of the Americas. Oregon became the "Friend" of Costa Rica. With this in mind, I told a Costa Rican I met at a meeting of the International Chamber of Commerce that ReTree was interested in helping them plant their future forests. We would get help from Oregon State University and timber companies. We would provide the trees and travel to Costa Rica for a special tree planting.

My offer was accepted, and I was able to get some seeds through the good offices of the local head of the Friends of the Americas in Oregon. He also gave me the names and phone numbers of people in Costa Rica who might be of help.

The U.S. ambassador to Costa Rica attended one of the first plantings we conducted there. That time we had planted trees outside of San José, the nation's capital, with high school students from the country's main high school, plus maybe two dozen Lions, all togged out in their orange jackets. I shared the platform with the U.S. ambassador and the school principal for a little ceremony before the planting.

Ralph Hannan accompanied me on one of my trips to Costa Rica. One evening I had a bad case of heartburn which went on until sometime after midnight, when I decided not to take it anymore.

I said, "Ralph, I'm gonna go down to the lobby and see if I can find a taxi to take me to the hospital."

"Well," Ralph said, "I'm going with you."

So we got dressed, and found a taxi to take us to a hospital. Since there were no English-speaking doctors on duty, I was unable to tell the doctor that I was suffering only from heartburn, or indigestion. Because of my symptoms and my being overweight, the doctor thought I was having a heart attack, and proceeded to check my heart and blood pressure and even to run other tests. Then we found a patient who spoke English, and he helped us convey the real nature of my problem to the doctor. He kept shaking his head and saying over and over again, "Ninety-three kilos, ninety-three kilos!" I have to admit that, at almost 205 pounds, I'm fat. But I've grown kind of fond of that big paunch—I call it my "baby".

In most of the countries where I go to plant trees, taking along seedlings doesn't pose a serious problem. Before leaving Oregon, I have them properly inspected and certified as being disease-, virus-, and insect-free. But Costa Rica is one of the toughest countries to get trees into. The customs officials want to keep the trees for a few days, in which time they can dry out and even die. But, as frustrating as the situation is, I really applaud the country for being so careful. I have seen firsthand what an infestation of disease can do to a forest.

Costa Rica has a seed center for the testing and growing of seedlings. ReTree has helped secure seeds for the center from the Philippines, Taiwan, Korea, the southern section of the United States, Puerto Rico, and other Central American countries.

One of these was Honduras, where we've also done a few tree plantings. About 1986, I went there to plant in cooperation with the Vermont Friends of the Americas. As Costa Rica is Oregon's sister country, Honduras is Vermont's. The Vermont Friends had hired a man and his family to live in Honduras and help with agriculture, to show the poor people how to live better. We planted trees with the Vermont group and local people near the city of Tegucigalpa. We tried to plant species that would help them, like avocado, banana, different kinds of citrus fruits, and others.

The following year, when we went back to do another planting, I asked the leader of Friends of Vermont if we could see the trees from the previous planting.

He just shrugged. "I'm sorry, but the cattle got in and ate all the little seedlings. There isn't one tree left, not one of the little fruit trees we planted."

In 1980, I wrote a letter to the king and queen of Thailand, asking that they permit ReTree to conduct a tree planting in their country. I explained who we are and what we hope to do worldwide. I asked that we be allowed to plant trees with their Boy Scouts and Girl Scouts, as well as American Scouts living in the country. A year or so later, I got a response from the Thai Forestry Department expressing interest in the project and inviting us to proceed with the planning.

So I went to Bangkok, Thailand, in the spring of 1983 with one of ReTree's directors, Dr. Jim Lin, and his wife. We arrived shortly after several key Thai forestry personnel had been killed in a helicopter crash. Understandably, the department was in chaos, so I turned to the American embassy for help. Apparently word of our project had preceded us, because the agricultural attaché knew all about it. He became active in moving things along, helping me to reorganize the project after the loss of the Thai foresters. I spent about a week traveling back and forth between downtown Bangkok and the Thai Forestry Department. The embassy supplied a car and driver, which eased the process. I spent many hours redesigning and writing details of the tree planting, and the Forestry Department freed some of their employees to help.

Early in my stay in Bangkok, I was advised to contact service clubs to help get participants to come out to the event. Because of my affiliation with the Lions, I naturally turned to them. The club there was a relatively new one, and they welcomed me warmly. They asked for a business card. I explained that I didn't have one, but gave them a blank check with my name and address printed on it.

One of the members said, "Hey fellows, this crazy American just gave me a check. What shall I do with it?"

I said it wasn't worth anything as a blank, and asked that it be returned to me. I wrote out a contribution for fifty dollars and handed it back.

The speaker at the meeting was a lady representing an orphanage in Bangkok which she wanted the Lions to help support. I got up and said, "Mr. President, where I come from, if there are two charities being represented at a meeting, if you give to one of them, you are honor-bound to give to the other. So I would like to add the same amount I donated to the club to this lady's orphanage fund."

A little later I stood and said, "Mr. President, I have just given you my life savings, one hundred dollars, and I think I have a right to the floor."

He laughed and waved me down. "Later. You'll get a chance."

When my moment came, I stood and said, "First, I want an interpreter. I came all the way from the United States, and I want your membership to understand what I'm going to say. I don't want to talk to a bunch of Lions who speak only the Thai language."

They all broke out laughing, since every one of them was fluent in English. So I charged ahead telling them why we were in Thailand, and what help we needed. Specifically, I hoped they would try to get people to the tree planting, and, of course, come themselves. I explained that the planting site was one hundred miles out of the city, but the cause was a good one, and as Lions, they would be serving their country well by participating. Actually, I never expected to see any of them again.

I had asked the Thai foresters how many people we could expect to participate in the tree planting. They said that because it was so far out of town, we might get one thousand to show up. They said they would set up a tent to accommodate refreshments for that number. When we got out to the site that Saturday morning, some of the people were already there. And they kept coming. Eventually there were about ten thousand of them! Young people, adults, old people. School children, college students, Buddhist monks, and several high government officials, including the Thai Minister of Agriculture. And all my friends from the Lions Club meeting, plus many of their wives and children.

I wanted the Minister of Agriculture to plant a tree, so I approached him. I was stopped by his aides, and when I explained what I wanted, they said that it was impossible, absolutely impossible. The minister would not plant a tree.

"Nonsense. Of course he will!" I insisted.

I pushed past the aides and approached the minister. I introduced myself and asked if he would plant a tree with me.

He smiled and said, "Oh, I know all about why you are here. Of course I will plant a tree."

So a retired nurseryman from Wilsonville, Oregon, and the Minister of Agriculture for the Kingdom of Thailand, knelt side by side and planted a tree.

We made the evening news.

I am not at all shy about asking anyone for anything when it concerns planting trees. I have approached the heads of major corporations for help, high officials in government, both here and abroad, and little children. We are all on this planet together, and we all share a responsibility for its welfare. Show me a person who is willing to get down and plant a tree, and I'll show you a person who understands that.

Like the president of Iceland.

In about 1981, I attended a convention of the Associated General Contractors in Washington, D.C. While in the city, I visited different embassies to inquire about the possibility of planting trees in their countries. Some indicated interest. Others, like the Republic of China, showed me the door.

One of the embassies that showed quite an interest was Iceland. We talked about some of the things they were attempting to do with their forests and the hardships that they had to overcome because of their rigorous climate. I was particularly interested in this because of ReTree's efforts to plant trees in Alaska. Here was another area, half a world removed from Alaska, where we might be able to do some planting in a marginal climate. I offered whatever help we might be able to supply—seeds, seedlings, whatever. The fact that they were already trying to develop forests for their future was encouraging.

When the first settlers came to Iceland, they discovered a land with many trees—mainly birch and a scattering of other hardwoods. The very first of these settlers are said to have been Irish hermits who came in about the ninth century. Their stay was brief however, and they left when pagans arrived.

In about 874 A.D., the first of the Norsemen, Ingólfur, established a colony on the site of the country's present capitol, Reykjavík. For the next century or so, a steady flow of Europeans, mainly from countries conquered by the Vikings, came to live in Iceland. Their holdings were large and scattered, with each homestead a self-supporting community. The country was considered a part of Denmark until 1918 when a treaty recognized Iceland's independence.

Eighty-five percent of the population lives in Reykjavík, the capital and largest city. There you can go to a restaurant and eat trout caught from a stream right outside the door.

The people were originally fishermen, but over time,

they bred sheep and horses brought in from Europe. Important as the animals were to Iceland's early economy, they were equally destructive to the country's trees, which they ate right down to the ground. When that happened, the soil washed away. Big chunks of it. Iceland has a bad erosion problem.

The island's name implies a very cold climate, but actually it has quite a rainfall and a milder climate than you might expect. It's caused by the Gulf Stream, I suppose. I think the future of Iceland is in tourism, since they have good skiing and other winter sports.

For many centuries, there were no roads in the country, just cart trails, so horses were the only means of transportation. Sheep, of course, provided meat and wool.

Today Iceland has good roads, but there are still fifty thousand horses on that small island. The Icelandic horses are small, a variety favored by Germany for breeding. Many farmers keep a hundred or two hundred horses on their farms, since they are a mark of prestige.

The country also has a small woolen industry and it is world famous. When I was there, I bought nice sweaters for my children. The Icelanders have tried to sell mutton to European countries, but they can't because it's too expensive to ship.

Both sheep and horses are allowed to graze freely, and they strip the foliage from whatever trees there are. While a few of the ancient birch trees are left, they are only a few inches tall, just a living shag rug. If there is any hope for reforestation, the planting sites must be fenced.

The people of Iceland take pride in the fact that they had the first constitutional government in the world. Iceland has many geysers, and the Icelanders have tapped them for heating their homes and businesses. They have huge greenhouses—heated by geysers—in which they raise potatoes, carrots, and many other vegetables. I've been told they even grow bananas.

Eighty-five percent of Iceland's income comes from the ocean. A large part of their fishing fleet is manned by Australians.

Though Iceland is a prosperous country, the people are frugal and responsible in their relationships with the environment, except for their horses and sheep. And agricultural officials say there are serious efforts underway to remedy that situation.

Iceland has a modern forestry department in which they employ some of the best forestry students from around the world, so they are taking the matter of reforestation of their country very seriously. Aside from the ancient birch trees, Iceland's forests have done well. The people have been planting trees since the late 1890s, choosing species they thought would do well in their climate. They selected Sitka spruce and other trees from Alaska, as well as species like Siberian larch. The two that appear best for the future are Sitka spruce and lodgepole pine. While they don't grow as tall as in the warmer parts of the United States, they do grow.

Since I wanted to do a tree plant in Iceland, I talked to their embassy in Washington, and about three or four years ago I got a letter indicating they were ready. I mentioned this to Dr. John Alden, the forest geneticist in Alaska, who suggested that in addition to a tree planting, we develop a major workshop on tree growth in cold climates that would attract forest scientists from around the world. The Iceland forest department agreed that this was a great idea.

Of course, funding was a major challenge. An international conference of this scope would be quite expensive. But apparently good ideas also generate solutions to the problems associated with them. At least this one did. When I was in Germany on a tree planting project, I discussed the Icelandic project with one of ReTree's honorary directors, Dr. Hans Franz Kopp, head of the German forestry department, and director for the forestry school at the "Georg-August-Universitat Gottingen". He suggested that I approach NATO for help with funding. I did, and NATO agreed to contribute help through their scientific division.

It took about a year to organize the Iceland workshop. Dr. Alden selected the scientific participants, and Robert Wheelon, a member of ReTree's Board of Directors, took charge of the event's overall organization. In Iceland, Sigugar Blondall, retired from the country's Forestry Department, did the organizing. I can't say enough about the work and talent that these men brought to the project. It simply wouldn't have happened without them.

The workshop took place in June, 1991, and about sixty scientists and foresters from twelve countries attended. Most were circumpolar, but we also had representatives from China and New Zealand. They represented a cross section of forest scientists interested in genetics and the effects of soil, wind, moisture, temperature, and just about any other factor that might influence the growth of trees in cold climates. The workshop's proceedings have been printed and will be published as a book in the latter part of 1993. Dr. Alden, and other scientists, think it will make a significant contribution to the study of reforestation and afforestation in cold climates.

Of course, I couldn't let such an important event slip by without including a tree planting.

Before going to Iceland, I looked in the Lions Club directory I keep on my desk. Along with the telephone book, it is one of my most valuable documents. I looked up Laugarvatn, Iceland, where the workshop would be held. They had a Lions Club, so I called the club's president. His daughter answered and I told her about the workshop, explaining that we would like the Lions to participate in a tree planting. She offered to tell her father, who didn't speak English. When I called back, the girl said that her father thought the idea was great and that the local Lions would be delighted to participate.

It was a great tree planting. All the workshop participants attended, plus the local Lions, Boy Scouts, schoolchildren, and Vigdis Finnbogadottir, the president of Iceland.

The President is a lovely lady, with all the grace and

charm of a true diplomat. She came out to our tree planting, and worked beside the children and scientists. After the planting, she invited me to ride with her to my hotel. Outside the hotel, a bunch of little children who had been at the planting came running up to us, and we had our picture taken together. That evening, at our banquet, I sat next to President Finnbogadottir. I wanted to avoid trying to call her by name, knowing that I'd mangle it, so I asked if I might call her Madam President.

"Oh, that would be lovely. I like being known as Madam President."

I said to her, "Madam President, I'm not trying to be overly friendly, although I am a friendly person, but I would like to have your name, address, and phone number."

She gave them to me, and since returning from Iceland, I have called her to help with another project. The U.S. Navy has a facility there, and it seems to me that half a million trees could be planted if Navy personnel worked alongside Icelandic children. The base commander agrees that they and the Icelandic forestry department could support such a project. So, maybe with some pushing from my friend Madam President Vigdis Finnbogadottir, it will happen eventually.

Chapter 20

Chestnut trees can regenerate themselves by sprouting. After the parent tree is cut, new sprouts will grow from the stump and roots. With proper care, these sprouts become mature trees, which can then be harvested. This has been the case at the monastery, Simonos Petra, where the monks have a large chestnut forest growing on monastery property. For several centuries, these trees have supplied the monastery's only cash crop. The monks harvest them, and sell the wood for fencing, lumber, and firewood. Responsible management has made this continuous cutting possible.

However, the Simonos Petra forest has fallen on hard times after European chestnut blight invaded it a few years ago. Foresters at the monastery were planting small plots of several tree species to learn if there were one that could replace the chestnuts. The species had to meet several criteria: Obviously it had to be compatible with the climate of Mt. Athos; it had to produce useable wood; and it had to reproduce by sprouting. The foresters thought they had found a tree that met all three requirements; the California redwood. Now they wanted to conduct a large planting to further test the tree.

I told our friend, Father Sergios, that we would be willing to bring the seedlings to the monastery at no cost, and he was delighted. Over the following months there was much correspondence back and forth between Old Harbor, Alaska, Mt. Athos, Greece, and Wilsonville. I contacted Louisiana Pacific Corp., one of ReTree's best corporate friends, who contributed four thousand California redwood seedlings to the Mt. Athos tree planting.

Along with Doug Coyle, a ReTree board member and the Director of Oregon's Forestry Department's fire control division, I made a survey trip to Mt. Athos. We discovered that another disaster had hit the monastery's forest. Wildfire had virtually eliminated the chestnut trees. The need for our redwoods was even more vital.

As soon as we returned to Wilsonville, I set to work. Scandinavian Airways contributed transportation as far as Athens, and from there, Olympia Airlines gave us cut rate tickets to Thesaloniki. The American Farm School offered housing for the few days we would have to be there, and most important, the abbot of Simonos Petra invited us to come. Without that, there would have been no project. In December 1990, we were on our way.

Athos is one of three peninsulas hanging into the Aegean Sea from the underside of northern Greece. Two of the peninsulas, Cassandra and Sithonia, are populated by farmers, fishermen, and summer visitors. Villages and farms stud the mountains like jewels on a thread, and are looped together by paved highways. The people have electricity, radio, TV, and other twentieth-century amenities.

Athos, however, is populated by about six thousand Orthodox monks cloistered in twenty-one monasteries. There is one short road from the port of entry to the capital, and it has a gravel surface. There is no TV, no radio.

A red line on the map separates Mt. Athos from the rest of Greece. In the fifth century the demarcation was more substantial. In 483 B.C. the Persian emperor, Xerxes, had a canal dug across the neck of the peninsula to shorten the trip for his fleet when they attacked Greece. Traces of it can still be seen.

The name, Athos, is a bit confusing. It refers not only to the peninsula, but to a six-thousand-foot peak at its southern tip. However, when a Greek mentions Mt. Athos, or more likely the Holy Mountain, it is usually in reference to the peninsula as a state. It is the only monastic state in the world and occupies the entire peninsula of Athos, a distance of about thirty-five miles. The first monastery on Athos was established in about 860 A.D., when the peninsula was dedicated to the Mother of God.

Legend has it that en route to Rome after the crucifixion, her ship was wrecked on the rocks of Mt. Athos, and she prayed to her son to save her. Because she was enthralled by the peninsula's beauty, she also asked him to give it to her, which he did. She claimed the land as a holy place, and decreed that no other female ever be allowed to set foot there. And that is how matters remain. There are no women on Athos, and there never have been. Well, that is not quite true. Infrequently, a few women, disguised as men, slip in to find work. When they are discovered, they are hustled off forthwith.

A visit to Mt. Athos is difficult to arrange and strictly regulated. Greek visas aren't enough to get one aboard. Without the letters of invitation from the abbot of Simonos Petra, our party wouldn't have had a prayer. But we still had to get Athos' visas, which Father Sergios was able to acquire.

We left Thesaloniki in predawn darkness, so I couldn't see anything. But from the speed we were traveling, I judged we were on a main highway. That changed as dawn was breaking. We turned onto a narrow, two-lane road winding through the mountains. Unfortunately, the bus driver didn't seem to understand the difference between it and the main highway. I recall careening along cliffs and around curves where the view from my side of the bus was straight down.

Aside from that hair-raising ride, what I remember most about the bus ride were the tiny, mountain villages. As we entered each one, the road narrowed to something that had been laid out when donkeys were the transportation of choice. Crowded up against the road were houses painted in brilliant, clean colors—red, blue, green, yellow, and white, lots of white. I didn't see one sign of life in the dozen or so villages we passed through. It was as though all the people and animals, every speck of life, had packed and gone. I never did figure out why.

It took us about four hours to reach the end of the road at Ouranoupolis. This town is a small fishing village and summer resort at the head of the Singitic Gulf, and is also the port of departure for the Holy Mountain. No arterial roads connect the peninsula to the outside world, and the only way in is by boat. When we arrived at Ouranoupolis, the weather was cold and a storm was moving in. The rain came on a bitterly cold wind, hardly what a person might expect based on Greek tourist brochures. Later, when I got back home, I checked a map and was surprised to see that the Athos Peninsula lies north of the fortieth parallel at about the same latitude as New York City.

It was at Ouranoupolis that I first saw an *arsanas*, an ancient stone tower on the shore. In early times, the peninsula was raided by pirates, so the monks built the towers as lookouts and places where they could be reasonably secure from assault. The tower in Ouranoupolis dates from the beginning of Christian times and is said to have successfully repulsed all attacks.

By the time the ferry arrived, the storm had hit full bore. The port was a quick turnaround for the ship, so we had just a few minutes to wrestle the trees and our personal baggage down the length of a pier, but we got soaked in the process. A loading ramp at the bow of the ship dropped open onto the pier. I half expected the Marines to come charging out. We sloshed aboard with our suitcases and ten boxes of trees. A small—very small—cabin barely accommodated the passengers. The trees and our suitcases stayed out in the weather. My fine old leather bag squished for a month.

The trip down the coast was slow, rough, and very uncomfortable. There were about thirty of us, all men of course, crammed together in the cabin. All but the five members of our ReTree party were workers at various monasteries. We were all soaking wet, and as the cabin warmed from the body heat radiating from all those bodies, the air got pretty rich with the aroma of sweat, wet clothing, and cigarette smoke. Everybody, except the five of us, was smoking. We had a choice—to stay inside and suffocate, or go out on deck and get drenched. Our guys stayed inside and suffered. I stayed inside and went to sleep. I'm one of the blessed people of this earth; I can fall asleep just about any place and any time.

A couple of hours after leaving Ouranoupolis, and with several stops at ancient monasteries en route, we pulled into Daphne, port of entry for the Holy Mountain. Daphne is a tiny collection of buildings crowded against the Aegean by a cliff that seems to soar straight up into the clouds. There our passports were taken from us. I never did figure out why, and Father Sergios wasn't much help explaining it. He did come to the rescue when a monk demanded that Allan de Lay give up his video camera. We had brought it to record our trip, and I wasn't about to let it get away.

"It's regulations," Father Sergios explained.

"We need a record of our expedition," I said. "We've got to keep it."

I kept chewing on the subject like a bulldog worrying a bone, and finally the camera stayed with us.

Simonos Petra is four or five miles up the mountain from Daphne. We got there in a Land Rover on a road built after the summer of 1990.

That summer, a wildfire had swept through the forest, compounding the disaster caused by European chestnut blight. To get fire-fighting equipment to the monastery, a jeep trail was dozed up the side of the mountain, and it was on this we were taken from Daphne to Simonos Petra. The trail was steep, narrow, and in many places covered by rushing water. By the time we arrived at the monastery's entrance gate, I was convinced that our driver had been a bus driver on the Thesolaniki and Ouronapolis run before taking his vows. He seemed to think the Land Rover had two speeds—stopped and flat out. That ride up the face of the cliff was one of the more exciting events in my life.

Simonos Petra is perched on the rock that gives the

we arrived, we climbed up a sloping tunnel that had been chiseled out of the stone many centuries ago. We emerged into a stone-walled foyer with a large opening overlooking the sea which was a long, long way down. Heavy wooden beams held up the foyer's ceiling. Against a far wall a wooden staircase disappeared into the floor above. We were led up it to our rooms, which were on an upper level apparently reserved for visitors. The only monks we saw up there were those who came to the sitting room where we attended several formal meetings.

Our party was assigned rooms that were furnished with metal cots, wool blankets, and clean sheets and towels. The route to the facilities was pointed out—through a door hanging eight hundred feet above the surf, then along a couple of hundred feet of planks lying loosely on temporary scaffolding. (The fire had destroyed the more permanent structure of the balconies.)

Simonos Petra, as all the monasteries on Mt. Athos, operates on Byzantine time. The day starts at sundown, and because that changes throughout the season, the starting time is changed once a week. The monks who lead an ascetic life, are up and about at all hours, working, attending church services and having their two meals per day. Of course, we were expected to adjust our daily schedule to theirs. Because we had no responsibilities other than taking care of ourselves, this different time-keeping didn't impose any great inconvenience, except for meals.

The monks eat two meals in each twenty-four hour period, the first meal and the second meal. These follow church services, and in fact are considered extensions of them. So if you want to eat, you had better get to church. To a person who has lived his life eating breakfast in the morning, lunch about noon, and dinner in the late afternoon, this schedule takes some getting used to.

My first experience with it was head-splitting. Sometime in the night I was torn from a sound sleep by somebody pounding rhythmically on a log. POK-POK-POK-POK, POKA—POK—POKA POK—POKA POK. Over and over. It began slowly and picked up speed as whoever was pounding got into the spirit of the moment. Then it stopped, and tiny bells, like Christmas ornaments, were rung. TING-TING, TING-TING. Rounding out the serenade, a cacophony of bells peeled in the darkness. Wake up call at Simonos Petra

Later in our stay, I was invited to climb up into the belfry to watch the pounding and ringing firsthand. What I had thought was a log was actually a beautiful timber, called a *kopano*, suspended next to the monastery's bells. Just the other day, Father Sergios sang out the rhythm over the phone from Old Harbor so we could get it into this book. POK-POK-POK-POK, POKA POK-POKA POK-POKA POK.

The church at Simonos Petra perches on the highest point of Simon's Rock. There is a tiny area where we visitors waited until a monk came out to escort us inside. It was like stepping into a jewel box. There were hundreds of candles, some in candelabra on tall stands, some branching from the walls. Hundreds more were suspended from the church's dome in an enormous chandelier. The soft candlelight danced on the gold and red vestments of the *euphenerious*, the officiating priest, and his attendants. The light touched the icons hanging on the walls, hinting of smoke-darkened, almost black images inside the burnished gold frames. One day, I expressed interest in seeing the church in greater detail. So, between services, a monk escorted us and we got to see the icons at close range.

There were no pews as such in the church, but a line of stalls circled the room against the wall. Each was large enough for just one person. He could lean back against the wall, or if tired, could sit on a tiny seat fastened to the wall. The services were lengthy and in Greek, of course, so I didn't understand any of the liturgy. But the singing of those male voices was magnificent. It filled that little room, echoing off the stone walls until it seemed to invade every part of the church.

I must admit that some of the more special services, such as those honoring saints, tended to go on at length.

At one point, I was getting a bit tired and thought to myself, "Why don't they finish up and get about their business?" My own thought came bouncing back at me. "This *is* their business."

When the service was finished, a tiny bell was rung, and we filed out to the meal, the clergy and monks first, we visitors bringing up the rear.

In contrast to the church, the refectory was well-lighted. The door opened into it at one end of the room. A rostrum stood at the other end. During the meal, one of the monks stood at the rostrum, reading from scriptures—in Greek. The only other furnishings in the room were plank tables and benches.

I don't know what I expected at that first meal, maybe some sort of ritual, certain formalities, perhaps pleasant conversation, and so forth. Wrong. The food was already on the tables when we entered. We sat on the benches and began shoveling it in, fast and quiet. We had ten minutes. The only sounds were the monk reading at the rostrum, the clatter of bowls and utensils, the smacking of lips, and discreet belches.

The food was plain, prepared in the monastery kitchen, of course, and in large measure grown in the monastery garden or taken from the Aegean. There were lots of fish, vegetables and fruit, cheese, bread, and cold water. But no time to savor any of it. The little bell rang and we were out of there.

Interspersed between meals, sleep, and church, we met officials of the monastery and talked with the three forester monks. Each of these meetings was introduced by the same ritual. A monk came into the room carrying a platter, on which were glasses of water, slices of an orange-flavored, sugar-coated candy called *leukumi*, and small glasses of a potent Greek white lightning, known as *ouzo*. Each guest was expected to chug-a-lug the *ouzo*, eat the candy, and wash the lot down with the water or coffee. After two or three meetings in a day, we felt no pain.

Father Sergios explained that the ceremony was legendary and was associated with the arrival of pilgrims at the monasteries. The *ouzo* was to dry up the perspiration from the journey, the sweet implied a sweet welcome, and the purpose of the coffee was singularly pragmatic—to keep the pilgrim awake.

There were about sixty monks at Simonos Petra, ranging in age from their twenties to one over ninety. They came from varied backgrounds: The old man had been a local fisherman, others had been farmers, and several had been attorneys, scientists, or educators. Most were Greek, but there were some from other European countries and at least one man from the United States. As I recall, the foresters were French.

We didn't get to plant those redwood seedlings. The storm lasted right up to the evening before we were to leave. But I talked with the monastery's foresters and was assured that they would take care of the matter. Many months later, Father Sergios told me that the seedlings had been planted, and that most of them were thriving.

Chapter 21

I've been planting trees for more than sixty years. I've planted them in city parks and in some of the most remote places in the world. I've planted trees in mountains and beside the ocean. I've planted them in one hundred degree heat and during Arctic blizzards, in pouring rain and days so dry, spit evaporated in mid-air.

I've planted trees with people, all kinds of people. Alaskan natives. Thais. Taiwanese and Greeks. Poles and Spaniards. Generals and privates. An admiral and an Indian chief. The president of a nation and a royal minister. Millionaires and poor people, many poor people. Blind people, deaf people. People with doctorate degrees, people who never saw the inside of a school. I've planted with people so old and frail they had to be helped to the planting site. And I've planted with children. Many, many children.

Why do I plant trees? I suppose if I sat down and really thought about it, I could learn a lot about myself from the answer to that question. I've been doing it for so long it is as natural as breathing. I can't conceive of *not* planting trees. But *why* do I do it?

Maybe the answer lies scattered among the words in this book. Maybe it lies, in part, in the time and place where I was born and grew up. We were surrounded by Nature in those days on the farm in Sheridan, and the little five-acre place in Lents. Although I can't remember giving trees any special attention, I'm sure I was very much aware of them. I played among them; I watched them come floating down the flume behind Harmony school; I fished them out of Johnson Creek. Certainly my sixty plus years in the Boy Scouts raised my awareness of trees. We camped in the trees, hiked among them, climbed them.

I have been a registered Scout for more than sixty years and have served in many of the volunteer positions. I have planted trees with the boys since those days of Troop 104. Those were wonderful times, and what I experienced and learned have stayed with me and helped steer my course over all these years. I'll be forever grateful to that fine man, Fred York, who served as our leader for so many years, and who, because of his own background as a forester, impressed on us the tremendous importance of trees to the earth's well-being. My experiences with the Stuart Rice Foresters went far to reinforce that lesson.

When I think about why I plant trees, I remember those little cedars that Mr. Lambert wanted destroyed. I remember how lovely they looked and how much I wanted to save them. And I did.

I can quote chapter and verse about what trees give to us. It's scattered throughout this book and repeated over and over when I speak to people who come to help at tree plantings. I plead guilty to personalizing trees in my little lectures, as though they consciously contribute to us. There's a lot of human-centered thinking in this.

A tree's gift to the earth is the result of the natural processes that allow that tree to live, grow, and reproduce. The carbon dioxide it assimilates is essential for food production. The resultant reduction of the gas is a fortunate plus for animal life, including our own. The oxygen a tree releases into the atmosphere, and which is essential to animal life, is just waste the tree has to get rid of. The delightfully cool air in a grove of trees that humans rhapsodize over, is the result of the trees' transpiring moisture into the air to raise water from the roots to the leaves. Hard, strong wood, so critical to human civilization, is the tree's solution to supporting itself and providing conduits for the transport of water and nutrients, and places to store food.

Pleasant as it is to believe that the tree "gives" us

anything, it's nonsense. This kind of thinking might be seen as innocent romanticism, were it not for what it implies. Buried under the surface of this approach to Nature is the concept of humans as "special," and that everything else is here solely for our benefit.

The truth of the matter is that we are partners on the planet with trees and everything else, and that we are all in the same boat. Over millions of years, life has evolved to the forms we see, and are, today. We coexist in relationships that are very much like a dance. A person has to move back a step or two from human-centered thinking to see this.

It has taken millions of years of evolution to produce the dance partners. Their relationships are never in complete balance, the partners are always changing. A slight long-term shift of temperature here, a drop or increase in rainfall there, and the dance and dancers change. We're included. But our human life span is so short we can't see the changes. They usually happen very, very slowly. It took 350 million years for the trees we have today to evolve from the small, fernlike organisms that began the long process.

In the slow, often awkward, evolution of species, the many forms of life on earth have merged into a planet-wide community. For most of the few million years humans have been around, we have recognized this. We passed the wisdom along in our myths and legends. We called the wild animals "brothers," and the earth, "mother." Then something happened. In the process of taking control of our lives, which was very important to do, we tossed aside something equally important—the recognition that we are a part of, not apart from, nature. We threw the baby out with the bath water.

As we developed the ability to manipulate nature—to plow fields and fell trees—we went beyond reasonable limits in that manipulation. We became arrogant and eventually assumed that all that stuff was put on earth for our benefit, that we are the masters of the universe. The Bible tells us that we have "...dominion over the fish of the sea, and over the fowl of the air, and over the cattle, and over all the earth, and over every creeping thing that creepeth upon the earth." I'd say that, on the whole, we have exercised this dominion poorly, more like arrogant feudal barons than as responsible stewards. Somewhere along the way we forgot to use nature's bounty wisely and to pass it along to the people who come after us.

I love to plant trees with young children. They are so straightforward. What you see is what you get. And what you get is an openness, an eagerness to learn and do. When you tell them why we are planting trees, and what it means to the earth, they listen, and understand in simple, direct terms. You don't have to talk down to them. In fact, you'd better not try; they'll turn you off. I talk with children the same way I do with anybody. And I make just a few concessions to their tender years. I try to have the holes dug beforehand to make it easier for them, and I try, as much as my poor old hips allow, to get down to their eye level so we can talk. (Did you ever try to put yourself in the place of a little child? All those legs you have to look at! A forest of them.)

People ask me how many trees I've planted. I honestly don't know. I suppose throughout my life I've been responsible for getting three million or so in the ground. That really isn't many when you consider how much there is to do, but it's a start. And the important thing about it, aside from three millions trees that might not have been planted otherwise, is all the wonderful people I've worked with. I often wonder if some of those children who knelt in the earth with me years ago still have the enthusiasm they had in those days. I wonder if they have gone back with their children and said, "Look, I planted that tree when I was your age. It will still be growing here when you come with your children." That's a comforting thought, isn't it?

Since I established ReTree International, the work has been more organized and efficient. It would be even better if we had the funds we need. But I suspect that is a

challenge just about all nonprofit organizations face—
how to do more with less.

For all the problems we have faced with funding and
getting projects organized, we still get them done. And I
must admit I'm proud that ReTree's work does get
recognition. As the organization's spokesman, I sometimes
get honors more rightly directed to it.

Recently The Society of American Foresters made me
an honorary member. The Daughters of the American
Revolution presented me with their 1992 Conservation
Award. A few years ago, the Boy Scouts of America awarded
me the William Hornaday Gold Medallion, Scouting's
highest conservation award for adults. And in 1990, I
received one of President Bush's Points of Light Awards.

Later the President was in Portland for a fund-raiser.
His advance man invited me, as a Points of Light Award
winner, to meet and have a picture taken with the
President. I decided to give him some trees, but the Secret
Service disapproved. No packages of any kind were allowed
in the room. The ladies weren't even allowed to take in
their purses. "If I can't give him these little trees, I'm not
going in," I said.

The advance man had had dealings with me before,
and assured the Secret Service it was all right.

"You'll have to go in last," they said.

"That's all right with me," I replied.

So I was ushered in. Mr. Bush probably had no idea of
what was about to happen. A balding, retired nurseryman
from Wilsonville, Oregon, with a face that could have
been hacked from a slab of cedar, and hands the size of
hams, limped up and shoved a crumpled brown paper
sack at the President of the United States. The foliage of
several small trees peeked out from the top. The President
seemed bemused, but rallied nicely. He took the sack
with his left hand, and extended his right for the *pro
forma* shake. Instead of a hand, he got a green cap with
the words, "ReTree" and "George" stitched on the crown.

"With our compliments, Mr. President," I said.

The memorabilia were passed to an aide; hands were

shaken, pictures taken, and the President went on into the dining room for the thousand-dollar breakfast.

The advance man invited me to attend, but I said "No, thanks. I've already eaten."

So I went home.

We want people to plant trees, and to plant them properly. To that end, we have published a handbook to help leaders of groups organize and execute tree-planting projects. I have included portions of the handbook at the end of this book.

People ask me if I ever get discouraged because of the forest destruction that is sweeping the globe. Of course I do. But as my mother used to say, "That doesn't get the baby shoes." When I really get down over the destruction of forests, I dream up another tree planting project and get on the phone.

The Maya Indians had a saying, "When you cut down a tree, you must ask its forgiveness. Otherwise a star will fall from the sky."

Maybe that's why I plant trees. We can't afford to lose any more stars or any of the other magnificent, natural things on our little, blue planet.

Appendix 1

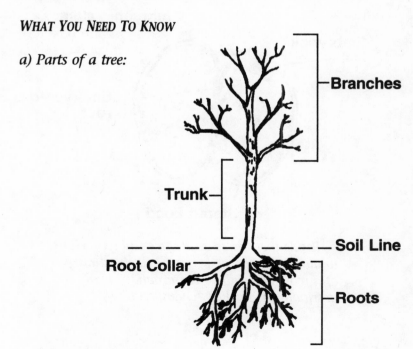

How to Plant Trees

Your site and time are arranged, as is your adult assistance, your sponsor, and your press coverage. Your trees are waiting to be planted. ***What do you and your kids need to know*** to plant trees successfully, and ***just how do you plant them?*** Let's look at the "what" first, and then the "how."

WHAT YOU NEED TO KNOW

a) Parts of a tree:

Branches

Trunk

Soil Line

Root Collar

Roots

Most trees grow from a seed (some sprout from roots of another tree). In the forest, seeds fall on the surface of the ground in the fall. In tree nurseries run by people, the seeds are planted in containers of soil.

b: How a tree grows:

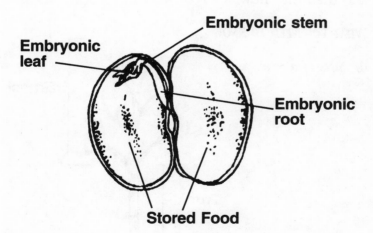

Embryonic stem

Embryonic leaf

Embryonic root

Stored Food

Inside the seed is a tiny tree embryo, with miniature leaves, a stem, and the beginnings of a root. The embryo is surrounded by a nutritious food called "endosperm."

**A cherry
seedling**

*As the embryo grows, its
root splits the covering of the
seed. The new root follows
gravity downward to the soil
as it grows. When it pushes
into the soil, it anchors
the young tree and begins
absorbing water and
minerals.*

*The leaves
emerge from the
seed covering and
photosynthesis
begins—the
amazing process
by which
chlorophyll in
green leaves
converts sunlight
into food energy
for the plant.*

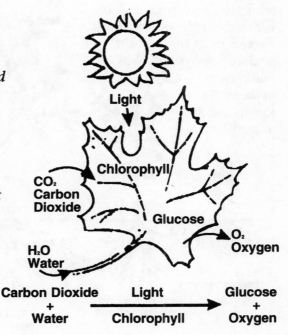

Trees grow upward from the "terminal," or end, bud on the tip of the stem below the uppermost leaves. (Jack had to ride the terminal bud of his beanstalk up to giant land.) New, live cells build on top of and around old, dead cells.

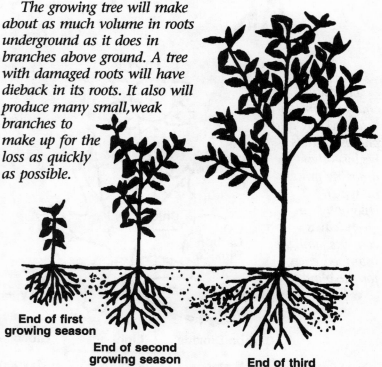

Terminal bud

bud scale

lenticel

this year

axillary, or lateral bud

last year

bundle scars

bud-scale scars

node

leaf scars

The growing tree will make about as much volume in roots underground as it does in branches above ground. A tree with damaged roots will have dieback in its roots. It also will produce many small, weak branches to make up for the loss as quickly as possible.

End of first growing season

End of second growing season

End of third growing season

Trees grow most of their branches and roots in the spring and summer months, then enter a rest period, or dormancy, when the coolness of fall sets in. The swelling of new leaf buds in early spring is a sign that dormancy is over and the trees are waking to another season of growth. Trees suffer the least damage when planting or transplanting is done in their dormant season.

HOW TO PLANT TREES

a) Site preparation:

How you prepare your site depends on the nature of your site. Planting trees in a logged-over area in a national forest will be very different from planting them in a city park or along city streets. ***Whatever your situation, visit the site or have it checked shortly before planting (2-3 days) to assess immediate conditions!***

Here are some things to consider:

- Thick grass must be cleared off each tree site (2–4 in diameter depending on tree size), probably by someone other than the children.
- Hard ground must either be softened by very thorough soaking, or holes must be pre-dug by adults.
- Urban planting may require pavement to be removed by skilled laborers.
- Compost (one shovelful per tree) is helpful to have on hand if circumstances permit (check with local farmers, or a zoo).
- Is watering required? If so, how will it be accomplished?
- Where will your group eat lunch, conduct educational activities and store plant materials out of sun and wind?
- What is the appropriate spacing for your trees on this site? It may vary from 4' x 4' to 10' x 10' (6' x 6' or 8' x 8' are most common in commercial plantings). You may want to mark each planting site in advance.

Tools You May Need Include:

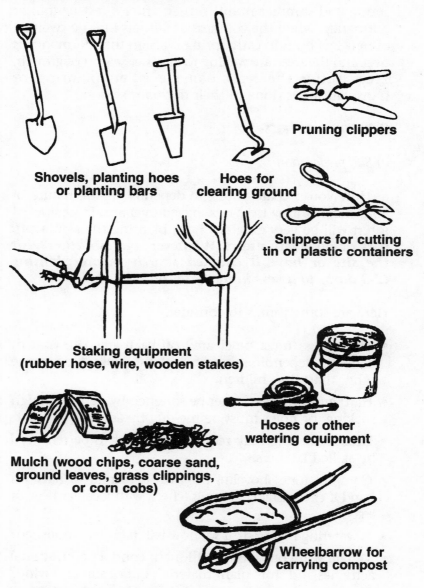

Pruning clippers

Shovels, planting hoes or planting bars

Hoes for clearing ground

Snippers for cutting tin or plastic containers

Staking equipment (rubber hose, wire, wooden stakes)

Hoses or other watering equipment

Mulch (wood chips, coarse sand, ground leaves, grass clippings, or corn cobs)

Wheelbarrow for carrying compost

Other equipment may include white canvas or plastic bags, or buckets for carrying seedlings; small stakes to mark planting sites; and tool cleaning equipment (brush, towels, squirt bottles of gas & oil).

We suggest the following organization for planting crews:

- Children in groups of 2–3 (one to carry seedlings, one to dig the hole, one to fill in the hole)
- One adult per 2–3 groups of children (help dig, quality control, pep talks)

Planting strategies vary for differently packaged trees (see illustrations on following pages). Here are some general tips:

- Remove containers just before planting (slip or cut them off)
- Carry bare root plants in a pail covered with wet organic material
- Prune off dead, twisted or broken branches and roots
- Be sure hole is big enough (twice as wide and deep as root spread)
- Remove all competing vegetation
- Check with a county extension agent to find whether local conditions require you to plant at, above or below the existing soil line on your tree
- Be sure the roots are straight in the hole
- Don't leave air pockets around the roots

b) Planting your trees

Your trees will be packaged in
one of the following ways:

**Containerized
seedlings**

Bare root seedlings

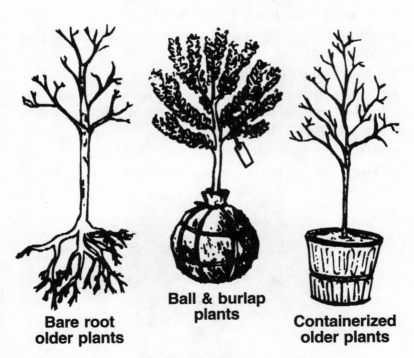

**Bare root
older plants**

**Ball & burlap
plants**

**Containerized
older plants**

Keep your trees shaded and moist *at all times.* If planting
time is more than a day or two away, heel bare root stock in,
and cover containers with moist sawdust or moss.

Planting seedlings:

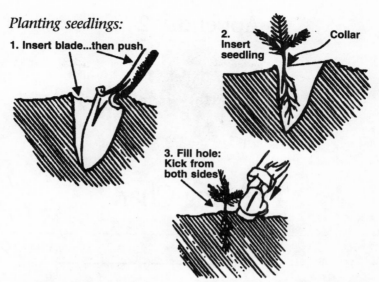

Planting older trees (bare root, ball & burlap, containerized):

For bare root older trees, dig hole twice as wide and deeper than roots. Soak roots for 24 hours prior to planting. Spread roots over mounded soil at depth it grew before. Fill hole two-thirds full; tamp every few inches. Slowly add one or two buckets of water: create a depression around the stem for water retention. Cut tabbed specimens free before planting. Balled and burlapped plants are wrapped; loosen cord and burlap before filling hole.

Appendix 2

Planning Chart

Planting Site:_____

Planting Time:_____

Tree Species:_____ Numbers: _____

Where:_____

How:_____When Acquired:_____

How Maintained until Planting:_____

_____

Transportation Details:_____

Sponsor:_____

_____

Adult Assistants:_____

_____

_____

Tools:_____

Provided By:_____

_____

Follow-up Maintenance:_____

_____

Educational Activities:_____

_____

Awards:_____

_____

Media Coverage:_____

_____

CONTACTS

Name	Agency	Phone	Address

Participant Checklist

____ waterproof, rough-soled boots   ____ working gloves

____ warm socks (2 pair)   ____ extra gloves or mittens for
                                                  dry changes

____ long johns   ____ warm hat

____ rain pants or dry change of pants   ____ lunch, including hot drink
                                                  or soup

____ warm shirt and sweater   ____ shovel

____ waterproof coat   ____ pail or large plastic bag

other items _____

_____

_____

_____

_____

_____

_____

_____

_____

_____

_____

_____

_____

_____

Appendix 3

Tree Planting Opportunities

CITY STREET TREE PROGRAM

1. **Find a site:** Look for areas in your city that do not have trees on the parking strip between the sidewalk and street, or check your city's street tree master plan to find areas that need trees. When choosing a site, be aware of power-lines overhead and of gas and sewer lines underground. Make sure maturing trees won't obstruct traffic views or block driveways or sidewalks.

2. **Coordination:** Contact your city planning forester (often in the city parks department) and/or your city planning bureau. You will have to obtain the cooperation of local property owners and tenants, as cities will not plant trees in front of a property unless residents want them and are willing to take care of them.

3. **What kind of trees?** Your city's street tree master plan will probably have designated the kinds of trees to be planted on the city streets. The species selected depend upon a number of factors including: visual effect, local adaptability, size of branches, maintenance requirements, and tolerance to drought, insect attack, and disease. Typically, maintenance requirements will be of the highest priority in most cities. If you are selecting the trees, you will want to research all these factors. In addition, you

may want to consider species that provide food for birds and squirrels, and to look at reducing spread of tree disease by planting a variety of species along each street. Most street tree programs use broad-leaved deciduous trees.

4. **Where to get trees:** Some cities have money budgeted for purchase of new trees, others do not. In the latter case, you will be on your own to either raise the needed funds, or to get donated plant materials (this is where having a sponsor comes in handy!). The trees will likely be obtained from local nurseries, so call around to see who might be willing to donate materials or sell at reduced prices (check quality carefully). Costs of young trees large enough to be used in a street project change by scarcity.

5. **Special Considerations:** Trees used in street tree programs are generally larger trees in ball and burlap or tubs. They will have to be transported by adults or older youths (a great opportunity for involving big brothers and sisters and reducing vandalism later!).

In some areas, pavement will have to be removed and rough edges finished off prior to planting. Your city will most likely assist with this. Make arrangements with either the adjoining landowners or your group for care of the young trees in their first year. Watering and some fertilization may be required to get them established in their new home.

FOREST TREE PLANTATIONS

1. **Find a site:** Much of the national and state forest land in the country is dedicated to growing trees for lumber production and multiple other uses. Large amounts of privately owned land are also needed for the same purpose. Where trees have been logged off, reforestation is necessary. While most of this is done by professional contractors, many forest managers hold aside a small amount of land to give youth groups an opportunity to plant. Contact your local, state, national, or private forestry office to find a site convenient for your group.

2. **Coordination:** You will need to work closely with the land owner of whatever forest area you have chosen to plant, as well as parents and the sponsor. If you cannot find a local forest office, contact state offices in your state capital or largest city. Officials there will be able to direct your search.

3. **What kinds of trees?** This will usually be decided by the forest manager. He or she will most likely select species suited for timber production that are native to the region. You may be given an opportunity to plant species that are rare or declining or that have particular benefits to wildlife, if you so request.

4. **Where to get trees:** In most cases, seedlings will be provided by the public or private agency on whose lands you are planting. If not, inquire about surpluses from the local county extension office and public or private tree nurseries growing trees for timber production. If surpluses are unavailable, you will have to undertake fund-raising efforts.

5. **Special Considerations:** Plantation planting often entails very long drives (up to two hours) over rough roads. Be sure you have clear communications about that with the forest manager and with your drivers. Vehicles should be able to negotiate narrow, bumpy, muddy roads.

Connect the first and last vehicle in your caravan with CB radios or walkie-talkies. This will ensure that the lead vehicle is aware of any troubles behind it.

Your group needs to be aware that the trees they plant on a plantation will be harvested in anywhere from 40 to more than 100 years, depending on the region and tree growth rate. This differs from other planting situations in which trees may be expected to live for hundreds of years, and may require some emotional adjustments on the part of the children.

URBAN PARKS AND SCHOOL GROUNDS
1. **Find a site:** The beauty, wildlife, and other natural

resource value of many urban parks and schools, colleges and church grounds can be greatly enhanced by the addition of trees. Converting grassy areas to forest also reduces expenditures for mowing and turf maintenance. Keep your eyes open for such areas that could benefit from a tree planting without detracting from other uses of the space, such as sports.

2. **Coordination:** Confer with the administrator of the area, as well as any grounds maintenance personnel, and interested citizen groups such as PTAs or park and neighborhood committees. They will all have vital interests and concerns regarding proposals to change the status quo.

3. **What kind of trees?** Is the climate wet or dry? Hot or cool? Is the soil heavy clay, light sand, or rich loam? Is the ground swampy part of the year, or well-drained? Your local extension agent, soil conservationist, or state forester will help you put together a list of tree species that will do well on your site. If you are not able to obtain assistance locally, contact ReTree International. Planting a diversity of tree species will not only enhance the natural resource value of your little forest, but will also create learning opportunities for your group. Be aware of which trees prefer sunlight and which prefer shade. Plant sun-loving trees in the center. Or, plant sun-loving trees in the first year and come back several years later to plant shade-loving trees beneath them. We encourage you to plant *native* trees that are becoming rare in your area, as well as trees that have food and shelter value to wildlife.

4. **Where to get trees:** Federal and state nurseries often have seedlings to give away to youth groups. Species are usually limited to those grown for commercial purposes in your area. For other kinds, check local nurseries.

You may also be able to get a permit to collect small trees from public lands, or from private land that is going to be converted to other uses (watch for construction signs on wooded land!).

5. **Special considerations:** Watering and grass control will most likely be necessary through the first year or two to help the trees get established. Vandalism is often a problem in urban areas. Involving older boys from the neighborhood (the most vandalism-prone sex and age group) will reduce any inclination they might have to destroy the trees.

STREAM, RIVER AND LAKE BANKS

1. **Find a site:** Many once lush vegetated streams, rivers, and lakes have been severely denuded, particularly in the west. Overgrazing by livestock, clearing of the land for agriculture, careless logging, overuse by hikers, equestrians and cyclists have all contributed. The result has been a loss of important wildlife habitat, an increase of water temperatures to the detriment of fish, sedimentation, erosion, and disruption of many streams' natural flow patterns. Spring flooding is worsened, as is summer drought. Any stream, river, or lake that does not have trees and shrubs along its banks is a candidate for planting. If you are not aware of a potential site, contact one of the agencies discussed below.

2. **Coordination:** The Soil Conservation Service, under the U.S. Department of Agriculture, is the agency with the most expertise in the Izaak Walton Riparian Enhancement Program (waterside vegetation). County extension agents, the U.S. Forestry Service and the Bureau of Land Management may also have local staff knowledgeable in this area, as may your state wildlife agency. The landowners, be it a public or private individual or group, must be in agreement with any proposed actions.

3. **What kind of trees?** Use species that enjoy or even require having their "feet wet," such as willows, spireas, cottonwood, dogwood, and bald cypress along the banks. Other species native to the site are appropriate away from or above the stream. Check with your local soil and water

conservation district, Forest Service office, or county extension agent for information.

4. **Where to get trees:** The Soil Conservation Service and/or the Bureau of Land Management may be able to provide rooted cuttings of riparian trees and shrubs. Cuttings can be made and planted right on the spot from shrubs in the general area.

Cuttings of many other hardwood trees and shrubs can be made in the fall and planted in the spring. Please refer to a propagation manual for exact instructions.

5. **Special considerations:** If the area has been denuded from overuse of some sort, steps must be taken to protect the new plants from the same fate as their predecessors.

This may mean construction of fences to keep out livestock, posting signs and roping off areas to keep out human abusers, and possibly other public information efforts. Coordinate this with the land owner. Plants away from the water may need to be doused regularly during the dry season to assure their establishment. Access to some sites may require a long drive over a rough road.

WIND BREAKS

1. **Find a site:** Many areas of the country suffer from strong winds that make life uncomfortable for residents and, in farming areas, blow away valuable topsoil. If you live in such an area, be on the watch for open stretches of land that allow wind speed to pick up. These may be farms, parks, treeless subdivisions, or large parking lots. Any such spot is a candidate for one or several windbreaks.

2. **Coordination:** The Agriculture Extension Service and the Soil Conservation Service both have extensive knowledge regarding the planting of windbreaks. Neighborhood associations in urban areas and Grange associations in rural areas could be very helpful in planning and conducting this type of a tree planting. Property

owners must be in agreement with your plans. If you are beginning an effort to reduce winds in your city or town, coordinate with your city planning bureau.

3. **What kind of trees?** The exact species will vary depending on where you live, but you will want trees with deep root systems to prevent their blowing over. The thick foliage of evergreens will block winds in winter as well as in summer. Tall, narrow Lombardy poplars, which may be planted closely together, are a commonly used deciduous tree. Per the instructions in Appendix 1, additional rows of low deciduous trees and/or shrubs may be planted.

4. **Where to get trees:** You may be able to get deep-rooting conifers from state or federal forest agencies (do not use Douglas firs!). If not, or if you want to use additional plant materials, you will have to make arrangements for purchase or donation from a local nursery.

The property owner may reasonably be requested to contribute some or all of the funds to purchase trees.

5. **Special considerations:** You will need to make arrangements for irrigations and controlling weeds around your windbreak for the next year or two.

OTHER OPPORTUNITIES FOR TREE PLANTING

1. Look for areas in which natural disaster has destroyed trees, such as around Mount St. Helens in Washington state, or hurricane Hugo and other hurricane devastated areas, or areas where floods or landslides have obliterated vegetation.

2. Look for areas where human activities have disrupted the landscape, such as agricultural land that is eroding and gullying, abandoned industrial sites or residential areas, water storage reservoirs, or strip mined and mine spoiled areas.

3. In suburban areas, organize neighborhood forests

along back fences and property lines, but let them be planted in groves and not a single line of trees.

4. Connect with a youth group in a foreign country to help instigate a tree planting there.

ReTree International will assist any group that wishes to contribute in any way to reforestation here or elsewhere in the world.